Mordecai Siegal's Happy Pet/Happy Owner Book

Other Books by Mordecai Siegal
The Good Dog Book

And Co-Authored by Mordecai Siegal
Good Dog, Bad Dog
Underdog

Mordecai Siegal's Happy Pet/Happy Owner Book

How to Recognize and Handle the Emotional Problems of Your Pet

Mordecai Siegal

Rawson Associates Publishers, Inc.
New York

For my son T. J.
How do you say thank you for the sunshine?

Permission to quote material from:
CANINE DIETETICS, copyright 1975 by
Mark Morris Associates, Topeka, Kansas.

Gaine's BASIC GUIDE TO CANINE NUTRITION
(Fourth Edition) by Robert W. Mellentin,
copyright 1977 by
General Foods Corporation, White Plains, New York.

Library of Congress Cataloging in Publication Data

Siegal, Mordecai.
Mordecai Siegal's Happy pet/happy owner book.

Bibliography: p.
Includes index.
1. Dogs—Behavior. 2. Cats—Behavior. 3. Dogs—
Training. 4. Cats—Training. I. Title.
II. Title: Happy pet/happy owner book.
SF433.S57   636.7′08′87   77-76999
ISBN 0-89256-030-4

Manufactured in the United States of America by
Fairfield Graphics, Fairfield, Pennsylvania
Designed by Gene Siegel
First Edition

CONTENTS

ACKNOWLEDGMENTS

For the excruciating silence and for the use of her imagination, I wish to express deepest gratitude to my wife Vicki, whose insistence and assistance brought this book about.

Thank you, Mark Morris, Jr., for the use of the hall, not to mention your research, charts, and other materials.

To Walter Chimel, Director and Patricia Davis of the Gaines Dog Research Center, for charts and other nutritional materials, I am grateful.

A special debt of gratitude to Shirlee Kalstone for her grooming expertise and generous attitude.

A special note of appreciation for the photographic talent of Susan Brooks of the Bide-A-Wee Home Association of New York.

And to Marcia Higgins of the William Morris Agency, thank you for breaking the mold.

To Sandi Gelles-Cole, my respect for your great editorial gifts and my gratitude for your loyalty.

INTRODUCTION

When a cat owner wants to pack a bag and run away from home because a dead mouse is left on the pillow every morning, something must be done. When a dog wants to pack a bag and run away from home because his owner wants him to mate with a strange female, something must be done. The emotional entanglements of dogs, cats, and people may seem very funny unless you happen to be one of the parties to the entanglement. Is Mickey Mouse asking too much of Pluto by expecting him to obey an obedience command in that funny little voice? You might as well ask a dog to chew bubble gum and snap it. Retire a cat who works for a living and watch her suffer a nervous breakdown. Try to thwart the lusty needs of a feline sex goddess and you'd better call out the vice squad. Depressed dogs and obese cats represent the tip of the emotional icebergs that can pervade an otherwise happy household. When cats destroy the furniture and dogs refuse to be housebroken, it's time to come to grips with their emotional problems. It's time to find out who your pet really is.

For too long the pet owner has had to stumble around

blindly in hopes that things will right themselves or else just learn to live with the unlivable. Unfortunately, fools and their pets are soon parted; and feelings, emotional connections, and even lives are squandered in the wake.

The answers to your pets' problems are as different and unique as one pet from another. There are no set answers to any behavior difficulties. The same problem may have to be solved in twenty different ways for twenty different pets. What works for one dog or cat will almost certainly not work for another. The pet owner might as well throw away preconceived notions, old formulations, amateur advice, and his or her own instinctive behavior. Where, you ask, does that leave us?

Assuming the relationship with your dog or cat is important, the solution for an emotional problem requires human effort and understanding. We must be able to evaluate a pet's behavior as being abnormal or normal—*for the pet!* All too often a dog or cat will seem to be behaving strangely. However, its behavior, which is genetically organized by nature, may be absolutely correct for that species despite the fact that it conflicts with human values. *What is required of the human pet owner is a working knowledge of dog or cat behavior so that elements in the environment which stimulate unpleasant behavior can be modified, eliminated, or at the very least understood.* If an animal's behavior is evaluated as abnormal when compared to its true nature, there is little the layman can do outside of seeking professional help. Some problems can be solved by professional trainers and handlers; others require the services of clinicians working in behavior modification. Fortunately, most emotional problems suffered by pet dogs and cats can be solved by understanding what's normal for that species and why. With that information, we can set out to alter the living conditions that create the problem.

Each chapter of this book reflects an important category that is of vital concern to all pet owners. In each chapter, the subject is discussed in the context of the emotional problems of the animal. This is immediately followed by a composite case study that best illustrates the plight of the animal and its effect on the human involved. Each vignette represents many combined people, pets, and situations. It is hoped that these stories will entertain as well as illuminate.

Before obedience training, before catnip and litter pans, before the retrieved stick and rubber ball with the bell inside, there is inherited behavior, genetically organized for life in the wild state. The evolution of dogs and cats never took into account the plus and minus of human intervention. Learning how to recognize and cope with inherited canine and feline behavior can make the difference between a happy or neurotic pet. And a happy pet creates a happy owner.

Mordecai Siegal's Happy Pet/Happy Owner Book

CHAPTER ONE

HUSHPUPPY NIGHTS AND KITTENS ON THE KEYS

Puppyhood

Once a puppy whispers in your ear, life is never the same. Baby dogs are like love machines whose mainsprings take a full year to unwind to a steady, rhythmic pace. A little wet nose, a slurping tongue, four paws, and a metronome tail click madly away in an indefatigable ode to joy. The puppy experience is like no other. To miss it is to miss the rainbow side of doghood. Although their tiny teeth bite like sharp needles and their piddling on the carpet is nerve-wracking as is the all-night howl of a homesick youngster, puppy pleasures more than compensate. The busybody waddle of a wide-eyed puppy and its cuddling desire to crawl through your armpit into your ear and lick out the last ounce of love is not only irresistible, it is addictive.

To understand your puppy is to understand the dog that he will be. There are those occasions when a puppy can get the most loving human into a state of frustration which can easily turn into rage. Understanding the little dog's true nature helps avoid destructive anger while you are finding solutions and answers.

As in human infancy, the early phase of a dog's life involves physical growth and mental development. Human childhood is a long stage, perhaps the longest in nature, and under the best circumstances involves two adult parents protecting, providing for, and instructing the child. Infancy to adulthood is compacted into one year in the life of a dog.

In the first three weeks of puppyhood, the young dog develops all of his sensory abilities plus many of his motor capacities. From the beginning of the fourth week until the end of the seventh week, the puppy enters a period of socialization the consequences of which affect his behavior for the rest of his life. During this critical period of socialization, the dog's environment plays a major role in how the animal will be able to adapt to human beings (and their demands) and the presence of other dogs. During this four-week period, the brain and the central nervous system are developing into full maturity. Interaction with littermates and the mother teach the puppy indelible lessons about "pack existence." This canine socialization helps them create attachments to other puppies and produces an animal that will adjust easily with other dogs as an adult. If, in addition, the puppy is handled by a human being at least twice a day between four and seven weeks of age, the dog will also adapt readily to humans with ease and comfort. Thus, by the end of the seventh week, the animal will become adaptive to dogs and humans and will get along well with both. It is then time to remove the puppy from the litter before the question of dominance and subordination is settled within the litter itself.

Beginning in the eighth week, some pups begin to bully others, while some become timid, shy and even terror-ridden. The issue of who is dominant and who is subordinate is settled by puppy fights, the competition for food, and best placement for the mother's body warmth. The largest male often becomes the dominant animal at the expense of the other dogs who in turn work out their dominant or subordinate relationships with each other. These placements in the pack structure become permanent in the minds of the dogs. If the litter remains together for up to sixteen weeks, the order of dominance and subordination becomes absolute. Often a dominant dog will become an overly aggressive animal, untrainable or unsuitable for a pet/human relationship. An undersized puppy may be last in the pack structure and develop into an extremely timid or shy animal which has negative consequences when he becomes an adult dog living as a pet.

Between eight and sixteen weeks personality based ·on dominance and subordination takes shape. In a pack environment, the young dog takes his place in the social structure until circumstances dictate the necessity for change. Anytime after six months, a dog is physically capable of mating and renewing the cycle. When a human family takes a puppy into their home, this cycle is still ongoing, with the human environment substituting for the canine factors. Ideally, a pet dog should take a subordinate position in relation to his human family (or pack). This can come about only if the dog is adaptive to humans and if the humans in the family take the leadership position (without becoming overbearing). When the pet owner understands this he or she is prepared for what comes naturally. In the beginning, all puppy behavior is based on instinct and the predilection toward pack structure.

------------◆------------

Marjorie and William Sweden drove 400 miles through the heart of New England to acquire what they hoped would be the most perfect Irish wolfhound east of the Mississippi. They had to answer many tough and demanding questions in order to pass the muster of the cantankerous breeder, a weather-beaten Mrs. Elvira Hagerstrom. "Will the dog be left alone much of the time?" "Do you have a veterinarian?" "Can you afford the dog's appetite? He eats a great deal, you know." "Will you attempt to campaign him and get him his AKC Championship?" "Do you promise *not* to mate him with a bitch not of his own breed?"

On their honor to do their best for God and the entire race of Irish wolfhounds, the Swedens felt as though they had just won a child-custody fight. Mrs. Hagerstrom of Baskerville Kennels reluctantly turned the curly-coated puppy over to the care of the excited couple, but not without a skeptical once-over that would have turned any first sergeant green with envy. The Swedens were now the proud owners of Baskerville's Juggernaut of Galway's Glen-in-the-Moss. They decided to call him Jughead— privately, that is, and about five miles away from Elvira Hagerstrom's icy stare. The large, sweet puppy responded happily to the call name. But the Swedens kept looking over their shoulders every time they said the name "Jughead." They expected Mrs. Hagerstrom to come flying at them on a broom like the Wicked Witch of the North. Little did they know that the flinty old breeder liked them and knew they would make excellent Irish wolfhound people. However, they had quite a lot to learn. There was much ahead of them.

The yowling and the whining seemed to vibrate all the steel girders of 73rd Street, east of Park Avenue. It was two in the morning, and the puppy hadn't stopped crying since the lights went out at midnight. Bill and Marj stared at the ceiling from their bed confident that they could tough it out. They read in a book that they weren't supposed to give in to the dog's whimpers, cries, yipes, barks, growls, or rar-rars. Jughead was an intense rar-rarer. He brought rar-raring to an art form. The puppy's high-pitched rar-rars moved upstairs from the kitchen, where he was confined, to the bedroom, where the unhappy dog owners suffered privately in the dark.

Marjorie dug her nails into her palms as Bill methodically ground his bicuspids flat.

"That's it," he muttered, rising out of his rosebud sheets like a bear leaving a burning tree. "If this keeps up, we're going to get evicted," he snorted.

Marjorie moaned, "We own the house, Bill."

"I cannot take this any longer. I'm going down there and I'm going to beat that dog within an inch of his life," he shouted as he struggled to find one slipper.

"Maybe a dish of warm milk will do the trick," whispered the exhausted Marjorie.

"What the hell are you whispering about?" demanded Bill. "He's not losing any sleep. The book said we shouldn't indulge the beast. No milk! Just a boot up his rear end."

Clad in his pajamas and armed with one slipper on his left foot, Bill Sweden descended the stairs of his duplex and marched to the barricaded kitchen doorway. He entered the room and frantically felt along the wall for the light switch. His pajama cuff caught on a picture hook and tore the sleeve up to the elbow. As the sleeve was tearing, his unslippered right foot stepped into a pool of liquid with a semisolid object in its center. His foot went sliding as his toes made a heroic effort to dig into the hard, permanently waxed linoleum floor. His trunk hit the floor with a solid thunk, and every part of him slid through the semiliquid mess. The stars came out for an instant, and Bill lay in the dark, staring at the luminescent wall clock telling him it was 2:17.

In a panic, Marjorie ran down the stairs and quickly turned the kitchen light on. Bill was still on the floor, on his back. He looked up at his wife as Juggernaut of Galway's Glen-in-the-Moss licked his nose, his ear, his lips, and his neck. Every inch of his pajamas was drenched in yellow liquid. His hair, right hand, left elbow, and right foot were thickly smeared in unpleasantness.

Marjorie laughed uncontrollably, Jughead wagged his merry tail, and Bill said faintly, "Help."

———————◆———————

Puppies do not cry through the first nights in a new home simply because they are willful or self-centered. A domestic dog's instincts are similar to those of his wild cousin, the wolf. If any wild canid should accidentally be separated from the litter or pack as a young pup, its life would be in grave jeopardy. The pup would be vulnerable to natural enemies. It would probably die of hunger since it is too young to hunt and bring down game for food. From the dog's perspective, the first nights in a human situation are fraught with terror. He doesn't know where he is or what's going to happen. Everything familiar is gone. He's been taken away from his littermates, his mother, his kennel, or the short-lived familiarity of a pet-shop environment.

In the few hours spent with his new family, the dog has learned that he is safe in the human presence. When they leave him for the night, his fear of the unknown and his need for mother's warmth gain control and cause him to howl. This is precisely why the puppy yells until he gains human attention. Unfortunately, that attention is often as unpleasant for the little dog as it is for the human. Too much howling usually earns a hollering or a hitting session.

Removed from his familiar territory, his littermates, his mother and even his new pack (the Swedens) poor Jughead felt lost and abandoned in his new home. Although it is not necessary to allow the puppy to sleep in the same bed, it is humane to soothe the dog and try to alleviate his fears. There are several ways to do this. The best method is to use a large cardboard box or crate as a means of bedding the dog in a confined area. Use a high-sided carton so that he cannot crawl out. *Place the box with the dog in it in your bedroom*

*each night so that the puppy is constantly aware of your
presence.*

This method is effective for two reasons. First, in the
first three or four weeks of the puppy's life, he has no physical ability to eliminate his body wastes. Elimination is accomplished through stimulation by the mother's tongue
as she licks her puppies' stomach and genital regions. In
those early weeks the puppies learn that no body wastes are
allowed to fall into their nest. The mother ingests them, thus
maintaining a state of hygiene. By the fourth week, all the
puppies leave the nest to eliminate independently. They
never relieve themselves inside the nest (if they can help
it). This imprinted behavior will be carried over into the
puppy's new environment.

Second, within a very short period of time (sometimes
within hours), your new puppy accepts you and your family
as his new litter (or pack). Therefore, sleeping in the same
room is very natural to him and brings into play his imprinted value not to soil his own nest. Jughead adapted to
the Swedens almost instantly and regarded them as his family with all of the behavior that accompanies that state of
mind. He did not want to be parted from them, but as long
as he was, it did not seem unacceptable to relieve himself
on their kitchen floor. After all, he was not in his nest, which
according to him was either upstairs in their bedroom or
back in New England with Elvira Hagerstrom.

Another reason for confining the puppy in a small box
is so that he cannot circle around with ease as he does before
he defecates. If you decide to allow the puppy's nest to be
placed in your bedroom, it is a good idea to close the door
just in case he manages to climb out of the carton. A free-
roaming puppy will use the entire house for his toilet and
may get himself into serious trouble. Because a puppy's
stomach and bladder are small, he may have one or two
accidents through the night, but at least the mess will be

confined to the box, providing he cannot crawl out of it. It may be a good idea to spread newspapers around the bedroom just in case the puppy does get out and relieves himself.

Another way of comforting a puppy so that he will not be too distressed during those awful first nights is to place a ticking alarm clock in the box with him. This simulates his mother's heartbeat and has some good effect. A half-filled hot water bottle wrapped in a towel may make it seem like one of his littermates is with him and also have a soothing effect. A dog's sense of smell is his keenest sense. Therefore, a towel or blanket that has the odor of his last home will be of enormous help in this distressing situation. Dogs remember many things by cataloging odors in their memories. The smell of their last home may be of great comfort. If the puppy is going to be confined in another room, play a radio on low volume or a one-hour recording of your voice on a tape cassette. This, too, may calm the little animal so that all may get a night's sleep.

———————◆———————

At age five months it was hard to think of the growing Jughead as a puppy. He was growing and starting to show some of the largeness associated with Irish wolfhounds. However, his awkward and gangling manner coupled with that funny way of cocking his head when viewing his first New York bug revealed him as the puppy that he was.

For the first two months, Jughead was never left alone. If Marj or Bill didn't look after him then the maid did. It was a perfect arrangement for a young dog until the night the Swedens were invited to a dinner party on the maid's day off. By now the canine adolescent had endeared himself to his owners with his gentle and affectionate nature. Like all puppies, Jughead was curious about everything and loped around the spacious duplex after anyone that would allow him to follow. Curiosity is the driving force behind all learning. When a puppy waddles away from its litter it is actually a sign of mental and physical growth just as a baby's crawling away from its parents the first time is the first step toward separation and adulthood. Jughead was a curious dog, but the Swedens had no idea just how curious he was. He had completely won their confidence as a good-mannered, well-behaved pet.

The large puppy was prone on the carpet with his face between his two legs, chin flat on the floor, as he watched his family switch off all but two lights. The evening routine was different, and the great puppy knew it immediately. His eyes swiveled in their sockets following the tall humans as they swiftly prepared to leave. The dog knew every detail of movement and action connected to the routine events of the day and night. Whenever the Swedens were going out, the maid was a presence and took charge of the dog's food and other needs. However, this evening the maid was nowhere to be found, and the master and mistress were on their way out. It was different and the dog knew it instantly. The gangling offspring never moved from his position.

Bill knelt down and squeezed the dog's face lovingly as he told him what a good dog he was and how he should protect the castle from marauders. As the elegant couple went smoothly through the front door, Marj said, "Okay, Juggernaut of Whose's Glen-in-the-Moss, be a good dog and take a long nap." The door closed and the dog was on his own for the first time.

At first there was no sound at all. After two or three minutes, the dog could hear a slight rattle in the heat pipe. He clumsily rose from the carpet and ungracefully bounced slowly to the kitchen to slurp some water and sniff his kibble. Having accomplished that, he plopped down in front of his food bowl and prepared for a nap as he was ordered. The dog almost fell off into a light puppy sleep, but suddenly decided not to do that and sprang to his feet. He checked his food supply to make certain he wouldn't starve. He was in a new state of solitude and there were no guarantees that he would ever see the Swedens again.

Jughead bent down into his bowl and ate two or three kibbles. But they were not satisfying. He felt like having something but didn't really know what. So he decided to eat the bowl. He gripped the large ceramic dish between his teeth and lifted it up from the floor. Of course, all the cereal spilled out onto his nose and then to the floor and partially into his water bowl. Noticing the slight splash that the kibble made, he immediately lost interest in what was in his mouth. He tossed the bowl to the side and jumped when it crashed into several large pieces on the floor. Once he recovered from that surprise, he fixed his attention back on the water bowl. First he sniffed it and then stuck his paw through the water to the bottom. This was very amusing, so he started poking one paw then the other in the water swiftly so that it splashed over much of the floor. The kitchen soon became drenched. The gray-coated pup decided to leave that annoying room because someone had made the floor uncomfortably wet and he was sliding around trying to keep his balance.

It was time for a chew on his white nylon bone, but it was somewhere in a pool of water in the kitchen. Jughead trotted to the front door of the apartment to make sure that his folks weren't standing outside waiting to surprise him at any minute. He sniffed the bottom crack where the door met the saddle. No surprises waiting there for him. It was time to explore and investigate those things that were always forbidden to him as long as some human was around to say no. He trotted to the arch separating the living room from the dining room and sat down like a sphinx gazing into the desert. His tongue hung out the side of his mouth and he panted as he surveyed the spacious room, deciding what to examine first. His panting stopped and he pulled in his tongue as the fringe of the Oriental carpet beckoned with its twisted, ropy fingers. They became a make-believe form of life that could be captured and eaten.

Big puppy swiftly pounced on the carpet's edge and tried to remove the fringe with his rotating paws. This was useless because the stringy material would not submit to his grip. With a high-pitched yowl, he lay on his side and tried to bite the elusive ropes, but they still slid between his teeth and lips. In a cheerful frenzy and with an expression that could be taken for a smirk, Jughead lifted the edge of the carpet with his paws and took a good portion of it in his mouth. This accomplished, he rose to his feet and began to pull for all he was worth. His muscles and bones tensed and set in place as a thousand pounds of biting pressure allowed his newly emerging canine teeth to sink between the expensive fibers of the imported antique carpet. An end table tipped over, one of the two sofas moved, as did a delicate wooden chair, and a porcelain lamp fell and unluckily hit the hardwood surface. The porcelain shattered when the bulb popped. Jughead dropped his grip and ran out of the room. That was the second time someone had tried to frighten him.

In a mad dash he re-entered the living room and attacked the arm of the tweed sofa. The pliant stuffing felt exotically sensual against his tongue and black lips as it twirled out of the shredded tweed and fell to the floor drenched in saliva. Jughead then hauled his bony body up onto the couch and sat comfortably on its soft pillow as he methodically munched the arm down to the inner wood dreaming of ancient wolves and Roman kings. And so the evening went.

Marj Sweden went faint as she managed to get herself to a living-room chair. Bill went to his rifle closet in the den hoping to catch the drug-addict burglar in the midst of his vicious assault on their beautiful home.

"Obviously," he concluded rather hastily, "they were tearing the place up looking for cash or hidden jewelry. I better call the cops. Say, Marj, are you all right?" He went to his wife as tears spilled from her eyes. She pointed to the opposite corner of the room and indicated that some-one was behind the large stuffed chair. With rifle in hand, Bill softly approached the forbidding chair as he silently unclicked the safety.

"Oh, my God," he shouted. "It's the dog!" Playfully looking up at Bill and Marj was Jughead. He had momen-tarily paused from chewing on the corner of the carpet—or rather, what was left of it. It was going to be another long night for dogs and humans.

We tend to classify the entire first year of dogs as puppy-hood. This is a very vague and general term which can be misleading. We must be aware of that major portion of the first year known as adolescence. For the pet owner, it is a sometimes marvelous, sometimes wretched period. Although the dog's entire nervous system including brain functions is fully developed by the third week, there is much to accom-plish in the coming months. Dogs are genetically pro-grammed with various survival instincts that do not take into account the good "pet life." Adolescence can be loosely defined as that period between the fourth and twelfth months. This is a period of body growth (twenty-four months for the largest breeds), sexual development and the refinement of survival techniques.

The greatest mistake the Sweden family made was to assume that their young dog was capable of being left alone in their home without supervision. Had they known better they would have had someone stay with the animal or simply have confined him to one room such as the kitchen so that he could not damage the rest of the house with his adolescent needs. In the kitchen (or other confinement space), he should have been left with his food, water, toys, and newspapers on the floor for toileting purposes.

Adolescent dogs left alone fluctuate between fear, boredom, and curiosity. Jughead had accepted the Swedens as a substitute for his pack. If the members of the pack leave him alone, even in the comfort of his den (home), it is bound to cause him some degree of anxiety and fear. This will lock into gear some of his survival instincts and be a great factor in his behavior until he is distracted or his emotions are quieted. From Jughead's point of view, how is he to know for sure that his pack is ever going to return—especially if a well-established routine is broken?

The first concern of a dog questioning his survival is his food supply. Jughead checked out his bowl and was satisfied. Although he did become playfully distracted by his water bowl, he felt somewhat secure about food. The next aspect of survival had to do with enemies. The slightest sound could mean an intrusion from a natural enemy or someone intending to violate his territory. This trait explains why a steam pipe noise could be enough to get an adolescent dog in motion. It could very well have been someone knocking at the door or even a telephone ring. All of these factors could have created a state of anxiety or fear which, in turn, sets the dog up for destructive behavior.

Boredom is probably the single most important element of unacceptable behavior in dogs left alone. All dogs become bored when left alone. Only the most well-behaved and those who have been obedience trained can be trusted to leave the house intact. Even then we are talking about a more mature animal. One solution to boredom is getting the dog a companion of his own—another dog or even a cat. Several toys that the dog knows for sure are his can be of great help. A good rawhide or synthetic material bone for chewing is good, as is a thick, tough dog ball manufactured for that purpose. Select a variety of safe, nontoxic (lead-free) toys. A young, curious dog is going to become bored faster and for longer periods of time than a mature dog completely familiar with his environment and territory.

Jughead's fascination with his water bowl was just another manifestation of youthful curiosity, an important part of play. We tend to regard play behavior in humans as well as in animals as a pleasant but frivolous activity with no more than amusement value. Actually, play behavior is a teaching/learning process for the youngster whether he is human, dog, cat, or other mammal.

All of childhood, all of puppyhood and adolescence, all of kittenhood is a mental and physical process preparing for independence and self-sufficiency. Even though pet animals have very little to worry about in terms of self-sufficiency, nature still provides the learning process including those involving play. When a litter of puppies or single young dog plays, it always has something to do with expending energy (exercise), learning how to fight (claiming territory, winning a mate, and confronting natural enemies), prey capture (hunting for food), or escape movements (survival). Puppies rarely hurt one another even though they bite and chew on each other as they roll and tumble in mad exuberance. However, a teething adolescent dog, bored and with a strong desire to play, can virtually destroy the home he lives in without meaning any harm.

First Jughead experienced a mild state of anxiety over the break in his routine. Then he quickly became bored. Next, he was swept up in a desire to satisfy his curiosity by exploring the forbidden areas of his territory and, last, he participated in play behavior that dealt a deadly blow to the Swedens' apartment. The fringe of the carpet became an exercise in prey capture, and the attack upon the furniture was a learning experience concerning attacking an enemy (albeit an imaginary one). Chewing up the couch and armchair can probably be attributed to a teething problem. It was all avoidable. All they had to do was confine the dog to one puppy-proofed room.

At five months of age, a dog may give the appearance of being well on his way to maturity—but that's far from the facts. For one thing the dog's twenty-eight milk teeth are slowly being replaced by the forty-two permanent ones. A youngster between four and seven months is in an intermittent state of teething. This can be a painful process involving diarrhea, poor appetite, depression, listlessness, and an intense desire to chew. When a young dog is teething, he is invariably going to ease the pain by chewing on objects around the house. Easing the discomfort is accomplished by providing suitable chew toys made of digestible materials, ice cubes, or a moistened—then frozen—washcloth to help ease the pain. Never give a puppy a chew toy that resembles a real object that you would not want him to chew. Old shoes and socks have the same bad effect. They teach the puppy to chew those items later, as a grown dog.

The Swedens might have been well advised to first take Jughead out for at least one half hour's worth of exercise before leaving him alone for the evening. This would have helped him work off some of his pent-up energy. Then a short play period involving tug-of-war or fetch or some other oral game would have been useful in satisfying his urge to chew. The single most important thing they could have done was to confine Jughead to the kitchen, after having removed all objects within reach including the power cords of appliances. They should have left him with his chew toys, his food, and his water. If the dog was teething, a dish of ice cubes would have been beneficial. Leaving the light on and playing a radio turned to an all-news station where the dog would hear a human voice for most of the evening helps. Had these things been done, the precious carpet, sofa, and porcelain lamp would have been found later that night as they had been left. Dogs—especially puppies and adolescents —have great needs, and they must be recognized and dealt with. The alternative is too awful to consider.

Kittenhood

Cats have a bad press when it comes to love, dependency, and expressions of affection. Don't you believe it, especially when it comes to kittens. A loaf of kitten, a ball of twine, and thou—and you are ready for more entertainment and emotional reward than you have ever dreamed possible. Although baby cats are capable of amusing themselves for hours on end, they would almost all rather engage you, the pet owner, in their frisky romps around the house. As a play/ learning experience, they will attack your shoelaces with great energy. They will jump on your lap like a mountain lion springing from the limb of a tree to catch a four-legged meal. A learning kitten can be fearless. That is what makes it so amusing.

Actually, there is nothing more demanding than a kitten looking up at its human family wanting to be held and petted. Yes, kittens and many adult cats crave loving affection in some physical form just as dogs do. Kittens however, are the needle-toothed jumping jacks of the order *Carnivora*. They cannot sit still for more than a few seconds and are constantly clawing your thighs for traction to launch them to the next object of play.

It may come as a shock, but your sweet, adorable kitten is a lot closer to its wild cousins in the jungles, mountains, and deserts than the dog is to the wolf. The cat has never really been domesticated in the sense that the dog has. Dogs instinctively live in social structures. Humans easily substitute for other members of the pack. But cats live a solitary existence in the wild and therefore are not geneti-

cally programmed to live with other creatures be they other
cats or human substitutes. It is only through centuries of
domestication, adaptation, and human bribery that cats have
gone against their most primitive instincts to go it alone.
Many house cats could easily revert to the wild state and
probably survive with a little luck. Even in domesticity, for
the most part, cats live as solitary an existence as circumstances will allow.

In their natural state, cats must hunt for a living, carve
out a territory, mate, and fight for all of these accomplish-
ments when necessary. These abilities are partially inherited
and partially taught by the mother cat's example and instruc-
tion. In the wild, the motivation behind the cat's behavior
is hunger, sex, fear, or anger. To this add a highly qualified
form of affection and dependency and you have a fairly
complete picture of the domestic feline temperament.

————◆————

Charlie Gaetano rescued a very young kitten trapped
in a broken drain grate in the basement floor of a twenty-
family apartment house. He was one of the busiest
plumbers in town and never grunted more than three
words at a time to any customer. The tiger-striped kitten
was all eyes and recoiled in fear as the powerful man
gently pulled it from its dark prison. The tiny waif was
coated with black sludge that shone in the light like a
domino tile. The plumber wrapped the animal in a greasy
old T-shirt that he used for wiping his hands, placed it
in his long, wooden toolbox, and closed the lid. The janitor
of the building asked why the drain was backing up, but
Charlie hollered, "Don' bodder me. Call my office you
want a report."

The volatile plumber went right home to his empty
widower's house and ran a hot tub for himself and his new

companion. He washed the drainpipe scum from both of them and cooked himself a pot of ziti with meat and tomato sauce. The kitten ate the leftovers. The large, brutish man looked down at the tiny thing on the floor as it looked up at him from what seemed to be a tremendous distance. Charlie couldn't help bursting into a large, from-the-gut laugh. He lifted the kitten by its scruff and held it close to his smiling face. The fur was still damp from the bath and felt just a bit sticky. Charlie rubbed his leathery nose against the cat's moist button and kissed it between the eyes. He looked into the little creature's face for a second and felt a deeply hidden emotion rush to the surface and spill a slight dab from his eyes. It was eight o'clock, and sleep was attacking him like a lead pipe. He was up every morning of every workday by six, and his muscles were never allowed to release their tension until after the nightly bath. Charlie yawned loudly and collapsed in his bed. In two minutes he was snoring steadily. Two hours later, he awoke suddenly to the crash of a floor lamp smashing into a large mirror mounted on the wall. Peering at him from under the sofa were two shiny yellow eyes.

"Hey, Minuto, what the hell you do?" The kitten crawled out from under the sofa, walked to the hairy giant in his underwear towering over him, and rubbed his body against the bare leg.

"Ah, I gotta get some sleep. You gonna do dis all night?"

———◆———

The primary activity of kittenhood is learning to survive in a wild state. (Nature never provided for the doting cat owner nor compensated for the pet-food industry.) Kittens learn to survive through the activity of play. Although it is comical and heartwarming to watch a litter of kittens hard at play, what you are witnessing is a lesson in fighting, hunting, and escape maneuvers.

Assuming that most play behavior in cats is a form of learning relative to catching a meal (for the sake of survival), then we can only imagine that different techniques in play are meant to teach how to capture different kinds of prey. Catching a bird is far more difficult than catching a mouse and requires different training. If a kitten hears a squeak or something that sounds like a chirp from above, it instinctively looks up and tries to develop a jumping technique for capturing the high-up source of the noise. Hence, a lamp has fallen because it was in the path of some higher source of sound.

Nothing is more fascinating than watching a grown cat after a moth or a fly. It simply follows the flying object around for a long time before it makes any aggressive move. The cat is studying the pattern of flight and landing so that it can predict where the fly will go rather than where it is. This is the same principle used in catching mice. Mousing is somewhat easier for a cat because the rodent usually moves along prescribed paths and routes and does not have enough time to adapt its plan to take into consideration the feline predator waiting at the point of entry or reentry. Some cats simply wait at the mousehole, sometimes for thirty minutes or more, knowing full well that the tiny creature will appear and be taken. But all this is hard-earned information learned primarily through play behavior as a kitten.

Cats are nocturnal creatures who hunt, mate, and work out territory in the dark. Kittens play at these activities through the night hours and cannot help themselves. All a beleaguered kitten owner can do is confine the youngster in a closed-off room with nothing dangerous available, such as a garbage pail or lamp.

It was fifteen minutes before midnight, and Charlie was in a deep workman's sleep. His snores could be heard echoing throughout the nine-room house. Little Minuto heard the sound and found it quite reassuring. As long as the plumber was making his grizzly sound, the little cat knew he had a free paw to go anywhere and do whatever he wanted. He also felt secure in the knowledge that his benefactor was around, even if he did holler and yell because the mirror was broken.

The telephone pierced through the stillness of the night with its irritating ring. The kitten jumped two feet off the ground at its first tremor. It must have rung fifteen times before Charlie stumbled out of bed, stubbed his toe, and ripped the Italian-language newspaper lying on the floor from the previous Sunday. He groaned as he made his way downstairs to the phone on the desk in the dining room which was heaped with unfiled paper and large steel tools encased in various degrees of rust and grease.

"Who da hell dis?"

"What? You crazy? I don' care you drown, it'sa midnight. I don't get my sleep, I drop dead ina morning. I know who you are. I know you my regular. Look, lady, you go down in da basemen, finda the main valve an' turn it all off. I be dere at seven tomorrow. Goddamn, dat's a best I do." With that he slammed the phone down and tried to deal with the acid that had risen from his stomach up to his chest and was making a beeline for his throat.

From the pantry behind the large kitchen, Charlie could hear several brooms and mop handles fall to the floor followed by something hard rattling around. He tried to clear his eyes and decided to go back to bed. As he got to the stairs he could hear the rattling getting louder and more pronounced. With full fury, he shouted toward the pantry, "What da hell you doin', you goddamn cat, you?"

The rattling did not stop. In a rage he stomped through the house and entered the little storage room at the back of the house and turned on the light. He looked down and saw his new kitten with a copper float-ball from his carton of spare toilet parts. The cat was rolling it back and forth and wouldn't stop at the large man's presence.

Charlie sighed and shook his head. He took a swat at the cat and shouted a horrible epithet in Italian. Minuto dashed under an old wooden cabinet and watched his master grab the metal ball and heave it back into the carton with a violent, angry thud. He looked around the room and grabbed a half-empty gallon wine bottle off one of the shelves. Seated at the kitchen table, the old plumber poured himself a large serving of red wine. There he sat in the quietly shabby kitchen graying with age and neglect, sipping wine. He was barefoot, clad only in his underwear. There were small holes in both tops and bottoms.

The silence was overwhelming. Charlie downed one glass of wine and poured himself another. He never once looked around the deteriorating room with its full accompaniment of dishes (service for sixteen!), dozens of large pots, kitchen and eating utensils, and near-empty food cabinets. He had half-finished his second glass of wine when he heard Minuto start to meow from the pantry. The kitten's call was not desperate, but it was insistent. By now a bit mellowed, he gruffly got up from the table and went back to the pantry to check on the little troublemaker. He had to get down on his knees to find the cat who was wedged between the bottom of the cabinet and some flat object.

"Okay, okay. I get you. Shut up, you little Minuto, you." With a hard tug, he freed the cat by sliding out the flat object. It was wrapped in brown paper and tied neatly with white string. With the kitten in one hand and the package in the other, Charlie returned to the kitchen and sat down at the table. The cat sat on top of the table rubbing against the gallon bottle as the plumber slowly removed the string and then the paper. Inside the neat wrapping, encased in tissue paper, was a silver picture frame holding a faded photograph of a sweet-looking woman in a velvet dress with a string of pearls around her neck. Across the upper right-hand corner of the frame was a silk black ribbon held in place behind the glass. Minuto jumped into Charlie's free arm and rubbed against his chest. His fur tickled through the holes in the underwear. The cat felt warm and good. Charlie held the kitten gently and stared at the old portrait as if seeing it for the first time. He sighed heavily, like the ocean tide going out.

The little cat pushed all one and a half pounds of himself into Charlie's face and was rewarded with a small hug. The phone rang. The old plumber downed the remainder of his wine, got up from the table and walked to the paper-stuffed desk. He picked up the receiver and answered, "Yeah? You can't find the main valve? Okay," he sighed, "I be dere in fifteen minutes." As he hung up, a noise came from the kitchen. The cat had knocked something over. Charlie smiled.

Because of the thousands of years of domestication, there are some major differences between house cats and those living in the wild. A cat living by itself in the wild is somewhat paranoid in its behavior and would fear every move made by any strange creature, including man. Even though domestic cats have the capacity to revert instantly to wild behavior when they have to and always live within a shadow of their own wild behavior, there are still dependencies that have developed. Kittens adjust or socialize to human handling and kindness and shift their dependency easily from a mother cat to a human benefactor. For these reasons, Minuto felt reassured in the dark by the sound of Charlie Gaetano's snoring.

Once patterns are established early in a cat's life, it is almost impossible to break them. Somebody opens a can of cat food. Somebody changes the litter pan. The cat becomes accustomed to these services very quickly in the game. Minuto had been rescued by Charlie, and in one day, the kitten attached himself to the gruff man whose need of the cat was as great as the cat's need of him. This angry, lonely man kissed the kitten. He cuddled it. He held it. Contact had been made between two beings and the kitten, because it was a rescued orphan, instantly accepted the contact— indeed, craved it. The kitten was too young to be off on its own in the wild or to reject Charlie and his protection.

If the cat had been past one year old and had been off on its own for a length of time, Charlie might have had a great chore on his hands. The cat would have done everything it could to get out of that house. But a kitten wants to be taken care of and to be made secure. Domesticity in pets is probably based on humans' constant appeal to the infant and adolescent aspect of the animal's nature. And so, to hear the man asleep upstairs is to know that he is there and that everything is safe despite his hollering and gruff manner.

Minuto was playing with the copper float-ball as if it were a toy. In the course of play, he banged the object into brooms and mops and made one hell of a racket. Cats and kittens play very hard with things that take on the quality of prey animals such as mice. They will bang the thing in one direction with a paw and then chase it hysterically and bang it into another direction. It's like army maneuvers— it keeps them sharp and ready for the real thing. For the same reason, cats keep sharpening their claws. Play is a serious business, but of course Charlie didn't know that. But a few hours' lost sleep in the beginning of their relationship was well worth the trouble.

The introduction of a kitten or a puppy into a household is often a rope thrown to those living in despair and loneliness. A pet makes so few demands and its emotional connection is so direct and innocent that only the most alienated can resist. A kitten needs to be fed, given a place to toilet, a soft spot to sleep on, and some direct loving attention. In exchange it will bring the natural world into the most artificial environment and restore the awareness of the human being's place in nature. When the pet owner understands this, almost any feline antic, no matter how annoying, is worth the trouble.

CHAPTER TWO

LEAN, SVELTE AND PORTLY . . . NOT A LAW FIRM (Food)

Dogs

Your dog thinks that eating is his job. If he is a normal, untroubled pet, he will eat your sweat socks if you cook them in gravy. Turning your kitchen into a fast-food operation for dogs is a great temptation when you consider the convenience of opening a can of this, a bag of that, and a pot-and-plate scraping of whatever. Emptying your refrigerator of last week's chicken wings and creamed spinach into the canine bowleroo only seems economical. Actually, a dog's nutritional needs are very different from human needs and should be dealt with accordingly. Although you'll get much disagreement from your dog, the point to feeding is to have the digestive system break the food down into nutrients so that the blood can distribute them to the body for growth and fuel. Pleasure and the many weird forms of gratification from eating are human traits not truly shared by animals. Our pets, if not made neurotic by us, eat only to survive. If they are not fed properly, they become vulnerable to a host of illnesses and live shorter lives.

The three sins of dog nutrition are too little, too much, and poorly balanced food. For full growth and proper functioning of all systems of the body, a dog requires a balance of protein, carbohydrate, fat, vitamins, and minerals. In the wild, this balance is achieved by capturing and devouring another animal. The first part of the downed prey that is consumed is the contents of the stomach which provides grains and/or vegetation. The flesh, the layered fat, and even the bones all contribute to the proper balance of protein, carbohydrate, and all the rest.

The dog's closest relative, the wolf, doesn't eat every day, especially during the long, hard winter months. Locating the prey and then downing it require a great deal of energy and exercise. When you couple this with the demands made on the body by the exposure to outdoor weather conditions, it is easy to calculate that the wolf or wild dog expends almost as much energy to work for his food as the energy equivalent consumed from the meal itself. One rarely comes across a fat wolf. Overfed or poorly fed domestic dogs lead shorter, unhealthier, and unhappier lives than those fed a well-rounded maintenence diet.

Among higher elevations in San Francisco is Telegraph Hill, where the fog is viewed below and the sun above. All of San Francisco can be seen from its hilly turrets. Near the top was a fine house partially hidden behind walls of shrubbery. A billowing bay window faced all of the city below and part of the winding street twisting close to the top. A constant fixture staring out at the breathtaking view from the window was a young dog named Antony.

He was the picture of indifference as the occasional Gray Line tour bus rounded the curve with its little windows filled with waving passengers. Antony always sat upon a red velour cushion tucked neatly inside a luxurious wicker bed. His throat was encircled with thick antelope hide hooked together with a silver buckle. His name was etched on a platinum tag studded with four diamond chips that dangled from his soft leather collar. Antony was part beagle and part scottie. He was an honored member of the Carmody family. Mr. Carmody was on the board of directors of a major West Coast bank, and Mrs. Carmody was the driving force of Bay Area charities, not the least of which was the SPCA, Antony's last known residence.

The sensitive, vulnerable Mrs. Carmody found the peculiar-looking dog one day while inspecting the euthanasia chamber. He just seemed too wonderfully ugly to have put down. It was love at first sight, quite luckily for the condemned dog. The society matron took the unfortunate creature to her home on Telegraph Hill and named him Antony. She lavished him in luxuries few dogs ever enjoy. Her attachment to Antony was swift and total. The dog's reserved demeanor proclaimed just the proper amount of aloof dignity that she admired the most. Charles Carmody understood very quickly that his wife Patricia adored her new dog. He never fully understood why she loved this funny little mutt when she could have had the most expensive specimen of any breed in the world, one with an outstanding pedigree. But Antony was all she ever wanted in a dog.

The rich young dog hardly moved from his cushion all day and was brought his meals in porcelain bowls as he continually stared out the window. The food was prepared by Mrs. Carmody's housekeeper and constant companion and friend, Aleta Barnes. As the elderly Miss Barnes adored her friend and employer, she also came to adore the standoffish dog with the distant gaze. Her personal concern for the dog was reflected in all her efforts for the animal's safety and well-being.

Antony was offered the finest cuts of prime beef and milky veal, not to mention broiled hen and dazzling omelets. At first the meals were discreetly placed next to his wicker lounge. He nibbled halfway through and left the rest. As time progressed, he left more than he ate. Miss Barnes then tried feeding the dog directly with the help of pewter tongs. Antony turned his face away with a hurt expression. Finally, Mrs. Carmody herself, with great worry, began offering small silver forkfuls with baby-talk entreaties. With soulful eyes, Antony would take four bites of food but no more, and that was merely a token of his esteem and appreciation for the good woman. Antony was just not hungry—or something.

Mrs. Carmody giggled and confided that she admired his finicky attitude. She felt it was more the discernment of an epicure who was used to better fare than was being offered. She told Miss Barnes that she herself had never eaten a restaurant meal that she finished and almost never touched the food at a dinner party. "Nobody cooks decent food anymore," she proclaimed in defense of the abstaining little dog. "If he could only speak, the poor dear, I'd ask him to supervise his own menu or at least select a chef of his own choosing." Miss Barnes shook her head with amusement. But Antony gazed deep into their faces as though trying to say something important. The futility of it all just caused him to sigh deeply in endured frustration as he turned once again to stare out at the city below.

It was Aleta Barnes who noticed the dog's loss of weight. She had a difficult time of it trying to convince Mrs. Carmody that Antony's rejection of food could indicate that he needed a veterinarian rather than a new chef. Even the most discriminating dog has to eat something every day. Mrs. Carmody halfheartedly conceded the point. "I'd rather he were finicky than sick. Call Dr. What's-his-name at the shelter. God, he has cold fingers." Miss Barnes smiled victoriously.

The chief veterinarian of the SPCA was summoned to the Carmody household to examine the dog. After a brief examination, he gave the dog a clean bill of health. The old vet did caution Mrs. Carmody that if Antony's poor eating performance continued, nothing could prevent the dog from coming down with something serious. It was suggested that the forlorn animal be force-fed for his own good. The idea of force-feeding Antony was so obnoxious to Mrs. Carmody that she seriously considered having the good doctor replaced at the clinic, cold fingers and all.

"But Mrs. Carmody, what are we going to do about Antony?" asked a worried Miss Barnes.

"Do? I'll tell you what we're going to do," replied the exasperated woman. "We're going to find the most important veterinarian in the country and have *him* figure it out."

A doctor of veterinary medicine was found in a midwestern university. Many professionals considered him the most important man in small-animal medicine. Pressure was brought to bear, and he was flown to San Francisco for Antony's sake.

Although the high fee and the expense-paid trip to San Francisco were attractive, it was hard for Dr. Triling Mansfield to take Mrs. Carmody and her problem very seriously. It wasn't until she offered to build him a new research laboratory that he took Antony's problem to heart. As a matter of fact, Dr. Mansfield assured his future benefactor that the problem could be solved very soon and that he was the one to solve it.

In two weeks between fantasies of groundbreaking ceremonies and ribbon-cutting celebrations, Dr. Mansfield tried every technique in his magical black bag to get Antony to eat. He started with a complete medical workup, including blood and stool analysis, X rays, electrocardiograms, electroencephalograms, and a complete check of the central nervous system. Having determined that there was absolutely no sign of disease, the ambitious doctor administered vitamin B_{12} injections along with

other appetite stimulants. Nothing. He changed the flora
in the dog's intestines. Antony continued to lose weight.
The frustrated veterinarian tried various diets including
one that involved brown rice and poached pork fat. It
offended the shaggy little dog. He was offered everything
from boiled tripe soaked in yeast and desiccated liver to
strawberry yogurt and meatball pizza. Antony would sigh
and turn away. With visions of his newly appointed laboratory blowing away like a crumbled sheet of paper,
Dr. Mansfield began to panic.

With the help of a San Francisco colleague whom he
offered a post in his facility (when built), he began acu-
puncture treatments. It was all to no avail. Antony was in
a deep state of ennui and just couldn't respond to the
slender needles and burning herbs. If they could only
understand his sorrowful gaze they'd know everything.
Mansfield did everything but a rain dance to induce the
dog to eat but he failed.

There was one final procedure that Mansfield wanted
to try, but it required the sophisticated equipment available only at Stanford University's School of Veterinary
Medicine. With Mrs. Carmody's permission, he placed
the dog on a leash and took him outside. They started
for his car when Antony caught the doctor by surprise
and bolted for his freedom. Mansfield made a frantic
effort to recover the dog. The animal was just too fast for
a man of his advancing years. With pale gums and
trembling hands, the ashen-faced doctor had to report the
loss to Mrs. Carmody, who promised him his rewards
in another life. Mansfield left the state with Mrs.
Carmody's threat still ringing in his ears about never setting foot on California soil again.

The days turned into weeks, and there was no sign or
word of Mrs. Carmody's precious pet. She and Miss
Barnes both grieved and were of a mind to consider the

little dog dead from malnutrition. Tears fell on Telegraph Hill, and a state of mourning fell over the grand house. Mr. Carmody decided it was time for his wife to let go of the past, so he took her on a Mediterranean cruise. He hoped she would soon recover from the wrenching experience.

The bereaved couple were at sea for three days when a call was received at their house. Miss Barnes clutched at her heart when the voice on the phone said he wanted to return a diamond ID tag and silver-buckled collar. In a flurry of pencil, paper, and stuttering emotion, she scribbled down an address and said she would be there directly. The man had introduced himself as Captain Jose Varagas and had told her to appear at the end of Fisherman's Wharf and to look for the vessel *Marcello IV*.

Miss Barnes never noticed the enticing smell of cooked shrimp and crabs or the large throngs of people milling about purchasing clams-on-the-halfshell and gaudy seashells with purple feathers protruding from them. She frantically searched for and found the *Marcello IV*, a scroungy commercial fishing boat approximately fifty feet in length and in desperate need of a barnacle scraping. Waiting on the dock was Varagas, an older man with a very gruff manner and the thickest, blackest moustache in California. Trying to avoid contaminating her dress with the smell of raw fish, Miss Barnes introduced herself and asked to see the dog. The captain informed her that he was the dog's original owner until his boat sailed by accident without little "Escudo." In his old life, Antony worked on the *Marcello IV* as part of the crew. He was a veteran of twelve voyages and earned his keep like everyone else.

The two parties explained their respective interests in the dog and tried to make their positions understood.

Aleta Barnes was quite prepared to take the little dog home, but Varagas pointed out that he was already home and should be permitted to stay there. He said that the only reason he called was the obvious value of the dog's collar and tag. An argument ensued over the dog's ownership. Both captain and housekeeper flared in anger. Threats were made. With the full weight of the Carmody stature behind her, she threatened to make more trouble for the captain than he ever dreamed of, from Coast Guard scrutiny to municipal inspections.

Suddenly she heard the dog barking from below the boat. He unexpectedly appeared on the top of the net full of freshly caught fish as it was being hoisted from the hold to the large receiving bins on the dock. The dog was dark with slick grime and fish blood. His fur was matted from the sticky fish, saltwater, and seaweed. He was not exactly the Antony Aleta Barnes knew who sat on his red cushion atop Telegraph Hill. However, the dog had gained close to six pounds and looked as solid as a pot-roast. His eyes were bright and his body moved with excitement and energy.

When she recovered from her amazement, Miss Barnes asked the captain what they had been feeding Antony—"Ah, I mean Escudo."

"Dog food," he replied. "Only the best, though. He's a funny dog. He only eats when he's happy and working makes him happy. Look, he's gonna get his favorite food now because he worked very hard on this voyage."

The first mate called Escudo over to him in Portuguese and made the dog jump for his coveted treat. It was a large fish head severed from an eleven-pound bonito. As the dog went to work on the unhappy object Miss Barnes tried not to be disgusted as she sighed with resignation. She then made a decision that could get her into a lot of trouble with the quick-tempered Patricia Carmody.

"Captain Varagas," she proclaimed, "I want you to take the collar and ID tag and drop them in the ocean the next time out. Will you do that for me?"

Varagas understood and nodded solemnly. Suppressing her sadness halfway down and twisting it into a knot, she added, "Give Escudo another one of those—things, you know, heads, for me and treat him well. He is a magnificent dog, you know." The captain agreed. "By the way, what does Escudo mean?"

The captain smiled revealing two gold teeth toward the back of his mouth. "Oh, it is Portuguese for one dollar. That's how much I paid for him."

She smiled and left the dock but turned back because it occurred to her that Escudo never once acknowledged her presence or even noticed her for that matter. She waved good-bye as the little dog took an indelicate bite dangerously close to one fish eye.

"Good-bye, Antony," she whispered with more than a little hurt.

One could hardly accuse Antony of being a finicky eater. His staple diet consisted of commercial dog food and an occasional fish head. It was the loss of his old life that took him off his feed. He would rather have gone into the euthanasia chamber at the SPCA than live away from his master, his fishing boat, and the other people in his life. The rich gourmet foods prepared for him daily had no meaning or value to him as a dog and were a complete waste of time. He probably would have refused to eat his normal diet even if the Carmodys knew what it was. Antony wanted to be Escudo once again and feel the deck of the boat under his paws as they headed toward deep waters. He wanted the life they had given him since puppyhood. There is a large difference between a dog off his feed and one that is considered "finicky."

A dog that insists on one type of food over another is usually involved in some neurotic game created and encouraged by a human. When a very young dog enters a human situation, it takes on many of the behavioral aspects of the environment, and that includes neurotic game-playing. When the finicky dog is fed along the lines of taste preference (the human's concept of the dog's taste preference, that is), then he learns to manipulate human behavior by eating or not eating. Some finicky dogs have been programmed to expect an elaborate set of food and feeding conditions, and if his owner forgets just one element of the pattern the dog refuses to eat.

Clearly this type of dog has been drawn into a neurotic situation which can only distort the true nature of the animal. However, it is safe to say that domestication itself is a distortion of the original life-style of dogs. In the wild, like wolves, they are drawn into packs. They must forage for food or strenuously hunt for sick or young herding animals. This means that they do not necessarily eat every day, nor does every member of the pack eat equally well. When a large game animal is brought down, the pack leader is the first to eat and takes the largest, choicest portions. But there is a natural logic to this behavior. The lead male wolf or wild dog returns to the den and disgorges a large quantity of undigested food for the lactating female and/or weaning puppies. Harder work and greater responsibility require more nutritional intake.

Domestically, however, dogs are not the leaders of their packs, nor should they be. A domestic dog is the one that is fed at the sufferance of the human caretaker who is, in effect, the pack leader. Domestic dogs that dictate the terms of their feeding habits are behaving in an unnatural manner considering their position in the pack (human family).

From September to March, wild canids are nomadic and

follow the grazing herds as a source of food. Between April and August, they remain within the boundaries of a fixed territory and eat squirrels, rabbits, small rodents, birds, fish, berries, and small fruits. Food is never more than a means to satisfying nutritional needs within the body. It has nothing to do with pleasure (in human terms), culinary art, aesthetics, or any of the social graces. Further, in the wild, food has no emotional or psychological meaning. It does not relate to love, acceptance, guilt, emotional stability, sexual behavior, or dependencies brought about through bribery or blackmail. These are neurotic values given to food by human beings. Unfortunately, some domestic dogs are taught to respond to them by their human families. This represents a clash between the animal's natural feeding instincts and conditions imposed on dogs by their human owners. This can lead only to neurotic behavior such as growling and biting over food; finicky behavior; withholding affection (gourmandise blackmail).

Too many pet owners feed their dogs as a means of soliciting their love and attention. Food is not love! Nor is it the currency of love. Allowing a bit of philosophy, love is an emotion requiring no qualifications or payments. It is either present or not. Heaping a dog's bowl with leftover roast beef, mashed potatoes, carrots, gravy and fat trimmings does not mean that you and your dog should buy furniture and take an apartment together. It merely makes the animal a four-legged garbage can of a love object. Dog owners must be able to separate their own relationship with food from their dogs'. Dogs eat to live and not the other way around.

Obviously, feeding a dog involves finding the most nutritional food available (a high-quality commercial food) and making no big fuss over its presentation. The same applies if the dog is fed a home-cooked diet with vitamin supplements.

Dogs that will not eat at all are usually suffering from

a physical ailment. There are those dogs, however, that go off their feed because of an emotional problem. Such was the case of Antony or Escudo. All that was important to the little dog was lost including his owner, his environment, his established diet, and, most important of all, his job. The most luxurious life in the world could not compensate for what was existentially the only true reality the dog knew. Many animals, including humans, pack animals and herding animals, will die in the face of plenty if they lose their positions in their respective societies. There is strong evidence that all animals are either given or develop a role for themselves in their social frameworks. When an animal is denied that role because of failing health, defeat, or alienation, he becomes a self-sentenced "lone wolf." This isolated creature wanders off in a meaningless journey from which there is no returning. Allowing a loved pet to eat like a dog rather than a human is probably more valuable to the animal's health than the composition of the food itself.

The nutritional requirements of dogs have been scientifically determined as a general set of principles. Each dog's body chemistry, however, is different and therefore uses nutritional intake in its own unique manner and style. However, enough is known to give every dog owner the knowledge to sufficiently feed every dog under most circumstances allowing for the necessary adjustments for individual dogs. Here, then, is a scientific compromise for feeding dogs made necessary by domestication.

According to Mark L. Morris, Jr., D.V.M., Ph.D., one of the nation's leading animal nutritionists and director of Mark Morris Associates of Topeka, Kansas, feeding a dog commercially prepared food is fine, but figuring out the exact quantity to give can be elusive and complicated. He cites the example of two laboratory beagles the same size, height, and weight. One dog can eat 20 calories per pound of body weight and get fat, while the other may eat 37 calories per pound of body weight and remain slim. In other words, the caloric requirements differ from dog to dog, and that may simply relate to the peculiarities of a given dog's body chemistry—let alone his environment, state of health, or activity.

Dr. Morris recommends that the dog owner make an eyeball judgment as to what is the optimum body weight for his or her animal.

Use the following general feeding formula and weigh the dog once a week to determine if weight is gained, lost, or maintained; then adjust the food amount according to the dog's need to gain, lose, or maintain weight. Prescribed amounts of commercial dog food based on quantities are not accurate unless you know the calorie count of the food involved in terms of a measured quantity. Canned dog foods vary in caloric count from 400 calories per can to 650 and 700 calories per can. Dry food will also vary, but within a narrower range: from 1,500 calories to 2,000 calories per pound. When you convert calories to measured cups, you must do it on the basis of the caloric count of the individual product, and that information is not always on the label.

When deciding how much to feed your dog, consider:

One can of average dog food will feed approximately 20 pounds of dog per day (based on 500 or 550 calories per 20 pounds).

One pound of dry food will feed approximately 60 to 65 pounds of dog per day. Five ounces of dry food will feed about 20 pounds of dog per day.

One patty of soft-moist (burger type) is approximately equal to ½ can of dog food. One packet will equal approximately 1 can of dog food. Thus, one patty will feed approximately 10 pounds of dog per day.

But dogs live different life-styles and are often in varied states of health. In the winter, an outdoor dog's caloric requirements may increase by as much as 40 percent. When feeding puppies, according to Dr. Morris, allow them to eat as much as they want during the growth period (from weaning to six or eight months, and in larger breeds, even longer). This is called ad libitum, or self-feeding. Always replenish the puppy's food bowl when it is empty. (Dry food and supplements are the most practical type for this plan.) A pregnant bitch should be fed her normal maintenance diet until the end of the sixth week of gestation. During the last three weeks, food must be increased by approximately 25 or 30 percent. During the six weeks of lactation she may increase her food intake by almost three times her normal maintenance quantity. This quantity must be made available for the proper maintenance of good health.

Refer to the following nutritional charts for further understanding of your dog's feeding requirements. It is always best to consult your veterinarian for definitive information regarding your dog's individual needs.

Guide for Caloric Requirements of the Dog During the Life Cycle

	Required Calories/lb. Body Weight/24 Hours		
	(15 lb. & under)*	(20–50 lb.)*	(60–100 lb.)*
LIFE STAGE			
Maintenance	40	30	25
Growth			
6 weeks	120	150	150
8 weeks	100	130	100
3 months	90	90	75
6 months	60	60	60
Lactation			
1 week	76	60	52
2 weeks	95	75	65
3 weeks	105	81	71
4 weeks	114	90	76
5 weeks	112	103	105
6 weeks	88	79	89
7 weeks	48	40	60

* Mature weight.

Vitamin Requirements and Their Deficiency Signs in the Dog

Vitamin	Recommended Daily Dietary Level/kg. Body Weight Growth	Maintenance	Main Deficiency Sign	Sources	Signs of Hypervitaminosis
A	200 I.U.	100 I.U.	Poor growth, xerophthalmia, suppurative skin disease, impaired bone growth.	Fish oils, corn, egg yolk, liver.	Seen more frequently than deficiency. Anorexia, weight loss, decalcification of bone, hypersthesia, joint ill.
D	20 I.U. (Assumes a 1.2:1 calcium:phosphorus ratio)	7 I.U.	Rickets in young and osteomalacia in adults Also lordosis, chest deformity and poor eruption of permanent teeth.	Sunlight, irradiated yeast, fish liver oils, egg yolk.	Seen more frequently than deficiency. Anorexia, nausea, fatigue, renal damage, soft tissue calcification, hypercalemia, diarrhea, dehydration, death.
E	2.2 mg. (Depends upon level of unsaturated fat in the ration)	2.2 mg.	Reproductive failure with weak or dead feti. Nutritional muscular dystrophy, steatitis.	Egg yolk, corn, milk fat, cereal germs.	None recorded.
K	Not required except during antibacterial therapy or chronic intestinal diseases		Impaired prothrombin formation, hence reduced clotting time and hemorrhage.	Yeast, liver, fish meal, soybeans.	None recorded but high levels probably dangerous.
C	Not a dietary requirement in normal dogs		Retarded healing, increased susceptibility to disease.	Fresh fruits and vegetables, canned orange juice contains about 0.5 mg/ml.	Nontoxic.
Thiamine	36 mcgs.	18 mcgs.	Anorexia, arrested growth, muscular weakness, ataxia.	Yeast, liver, whole grains.	No toxic effect with moderate overdosage.
Ribo- flavin	.08 mg.	.04 mg.	Dry scaly skin, erythema of hind legs and chest, muscular weakness in hind quarters, anemia, sudden death.	Milk, yeast and whole grains; dextrin, cornstarch favor synthesis.	Nontoxic even in large amounts.

| Vitamin | Recommended Daily Dietary Level/kg. Body Weight | | Main Deficiency Sign | Sources | Signs of Hypervitaminos |
	Growth	Maintenance			
Niacin	400 mcgs.	220 mcgs.	"Black tongue," i.e., anorexia, weight loss, diarrhea, anemia, reddening and ulceration of mucous membranes of mouth and tongue, death.	Whole grains, yeast, meat, scraps, tankage, fish meal, eggs. Tryptophan for synthesis.	Dilation of blood vessel itching, burning of skin
Pyridoxine	44 mcgs.	22 mcgs.	Microcytic hypochromic anemia, high serum iron and atherosclerosis.	Whole grains, milk, meat, fish, yeast, liver.	No toxicity data has been reported.
Pantothenic Acid	200 mcgs.	50 mcgs.	Anorexia, hypoglycemia, hypochloremia, BUN increase, gastritis, enteritis, convulsions, coma and death.	Yeast, dairy products, liver, rice.	No data available.
Folic Acid	8.8. mcgs.	4.4 mcgs.	Hypoplasia of bone marrow, hypochromic microcytic anemia, glossitis.	Yeast, liver.	Nontoxic.
Biotin	NONE on natural diets. Deficiency usually associated with feeding of raw eggs.		Tension, aimless wandering, spasticity of hind legs, progressive paralysis.	Liver, kidney, milk, egg yolk, yeast.	Nontoxic.
Cobalamin (B12)	1 mcg.	0.7 mcg.	Anemia	Liver, fish meal, meat scraps, dairy products.	Nontoxic.
Choline	55 mg.	—	Fatty infiltration of liver, increase in plasma phosphatase, decrease in plasma protein, prothrombin time, hemoglobin and P.C.V. values.	Yeast, liver, meat scraps, soybean oil, egg yolk.	Persistent diarrhea caused by 10 gms/day or greater.

Mineral Requirements and Their Deficiency Signs in the Dog

Mineral	Recommended Dietary Level	Common Sources	Common Deficiency Signs
Calcium	1.0%	Steamed bone meal Dicalcium phosphate Ground green bone Ground oyster shell	Enlarged epiphysis of long bones and ribs, splaying of toes, hyperextension of the carpus and tarsus, spontaneous fractures and abnormal deviation of the legs.*
Phosphorus	0.9%	Steamed bone meal Dicalcium phosphate Ground green bone	Same as above*
Sodium Chloride	Not required as such	Table salt	Deficiency is rare. Natural feedstuffs contain adequate amounts. When the deficiency occurs, weight loss, hair loss, acidosis and eventually death may be seen.
Potassium	0.8%	Potassium chloride	Deficiency is rare. Natural feedstuffs contain adequate amounts. When the deficiency occurs, ascending paralysis, depressed reflexes may be seen.
Magnesium	0.1%	Manganese carbonate Magnesium oxide Magnesium sulfate	Retarded growth, spreading of toes and hyperextension of carpus and tarsus, hyperirritability, convulsions, soft tissue calcification, enlargement of the epiphysis of long bones.*
	mg./lb. of food		
Iron	25.0	Iron carbonate Iron sulfate	Microcytic-hypochromic anemia, anisocytosis and poikilocytosis of erythrocytes.
Manganese	2.2	Manganese oxide Manganese carbonate Manganese sulfate	Deficiency is rare. Crooked, shortened soft bones may be seen.*
Copper	3.5	Copper sulfate Copper carbonate Copper oxide	Reduction in erythrocytes, swelling of ends of long bones, hyperextension of carpus.*
Cobalt	1.0	Cobalt chloride Cobalt carbonate	Normocytic-normochromic anemia.
Zinc	2.2	Zinc oxide	Deficiency is rare. Natural feedstuffs contain adequate amounts except when extreme calcium supplementation is attempted by overzealous dog owners.
Iodine	0.7	Iodized salt Sodium iodide Potassium iodide	Dead or goitrous pups. Erythematous dermatitis.

*Deficiency signs of calcium, phosphorus, vitamin D, magnesium, manganese or copper deficiency may be difficult or impossible to differentiate clinically.

Cats

Although domestic cats are referred to by many experts as "occasional feeders," it is astonishing to see the average feline's reaction to the sound of the electric can-opener. It is quite possible to lose a finger or two when "occasionally" placing a bit of freshly cooked meat in her plate, especially if it's a between-meal snack. Food is serious business to a cat. In both natural and domestic settings the cat's primary concern seems to be eating—or not eating—what you serve. Cats in the wild do not *eat* (a human term), but rather, they *feed*. Eating implies a hot meal served in comfort and taken in an atmosphere of safety. Feeding, on the other hand, suggests nutritional intake when and how it can be achieved. The house cat simply sits on the kitchen counter like a doorstop and waits for the food to be spooned into the dish. The wild cat must wait for dusk and then stalk an unsuspecting animal. It attacks and kills in a rush of energy that almost requires more fuel than the food value of the prey. By then it is the dark of night and the feline hunter must sit and consume its meal before a larger predator finds it and offers a challenge. That's *feeding* in the most stark sense of the word. Cats can be more finicky than dogs and sometimes give their owners a very difficult time. Dealing with a domestic cat's eating whims is difficult and complex.

In the wild, cats feed only when the food is available. Consequently, they eat as much as they possibly can at each feeding as a means of tiding themselves over until the next meal is captured. This habit often carries over to the domestic cat, who may overeat even though it is not really hungry. Many such behaviorisms of domestic cats are rooted in the inherited realities of their wild counterparts.

However, all cat behavior is not instinctive. A great deal of the domestic cat's feeding behavior is learned and often countermands genetically imposed tendencies. This is the result of domesticity, or the emulation of human behavior. Domesticity imposes an environment that often contradicts instinctive behavior, such as food provided daily as opposed to the drive to hunt, kill, and eat. Much of a cat's natural behavior is derived from lessons given by its mother during the period of kittenhood. The longer a kitten is with its mother, the more it imitates her behavior. And finally, human behavior in the presence of a cat can and does impose the greatest influence. Despite their own instincts, cats will develop responses to human behavior that are all too often unnatural or inconsistent with the genetic plan. That is probably why there are so many fat cats living with humans.

———◆———

For a cat, Sara Lee was fatter than most. Her weight was just under twelve pounds. She was an exquisite Sealpoint Himalayan living in New Jersey under an assumed name. Her true identity was Ta Nook's Mocha Pearls of Burnt Orange Farms and she was the daughter of Grand Champion parents who fell upon hard times. Her blue eyes and near-perfect sitting posture could win her a meal from just about anyone, and very often did. She was very like her mistress, Jane Springfield, who was recently separated from her husband, Alexander. For both ladies, life was just a long, boring void between delayed meals. The beautiful cat wore her avoirdupois well beneath her long, powdery coat. But her body was massive and undulated with every predatory step. When she stalked an outdoor prey, she resembled an oversized loaf of raisin bread. It is hard to know if Sara Lee was constantly hungry, but she did eat at every opportunity. She ate everything from canned kidneys in cream sauce to chocolate cake and an occasional thing that tried to get away.

This cat's view of the human condition was somewhat perverse in that she reveled with purring joy at the sound of her mistress's crying. When tears dripped from Jane's face, Sara Lee knew she could expect a warm slice of something warm and loving from the oven or a couple of dollops of something cold, sweet, and creamy. That her shoulders were starting to ache at the end of each day had no bearing on anything. And, of course, the tubby cat was just a wee bit slower in the chase and got out of breath more quickly than six months before when there was a Mr. Springfield in her life. Jane hadn't even noticed her own clothing tightening up, much less her cat's failing health. Sara Lee was just too hungry a cat to care about it, and so was her owner.

Although Jane Springfield never knew it, Sara Lee was about to lose her good health completely because of her obesity. She was precariously close to developing diabetes. It was about that time that Alex Springfield called his wife and asked her out to dinner. Paradoxically, the last thing that Jane was interested in was a good meal.

The date was set for three days after the call, and the exuberant Mrs. Springfield tried on every item of clothing she owned. To her shock, nothing fit—at least nothing fit well enough to get the correct effect. She went on a forty-eight-hour submarine dive of a diet that she had gotten from *Cosmo* or *Harper's Bazaar* or some such source. It involved New Zealand kiwi fruit and kelp. By the time three days rolled by, she had shed those important few pounds needed to get back into a size 12 strapless. Of course, the fact that she ate almost nothing and got more exercise running to the hairdresser, the dress boutique, the shoe store, etc. than she had had in six months, had much to do with her success. Most significantly, Sara Lee lost a few ounces, too. There just wasn't enough time for all that ice cream and liver and baked caramel. Diabetes was staved off . . . for a while.

The supper date was a great success. After six years of marriage and six months of separation, Jane and Alex still made an attractive couple who obviously cared a great deal for each other. The evening was a romantic one. They had drinks and a fine meal. After dinner they sat in their private corner of the restaurant, the envy of many, and discussed their differences, interspersed between funny tales of loneliness and absurd attempts to fill the empty six months. They had their brandy and coffee, and Jane even offered to smoke one of Alex's cigars as a sign of reconciliation. He declined the offer and took her hand in his and said, "Can I come home?" Jane smiled with a closed mouth to hold back her tears and nodded as she looked down at the table. Sara Lee lost her spot on the bed.

As a matter of fact, Sara Lee lost her huge granola breakfasts, her mid-morning danish, her crabmeat and avocado lunches, her late-afternoon egg salad on Ritz crackers, not to mention her chicken livers sautéed in sherry dinners followed by a nightcap of raspberry sherbet or chocolate mousse. Her dry Kitty-Poo meal was always in the bowl so Jane didn't have to feel guilty. What with Alex back in the house, Sara Lee had to settle for Kitty-Poo and a random plate of brown stuff out of the can. Despite the fact that the brown cat was losing weight, just like her mistress, she complained like mad. At seven every morning she ran from the bedroom to the kitchen meowing her oriental caterwaul in that irritating way that inspired Alex to throw a shoe every now and again.

In six weeks Sara Lee was down to nine pounds and was giving the local mice hell. She slept better and moved faster. It was about that time that the bickering between Jane and Alex began. By the seventh week, the bickering was turning to full-scale quarreling, and Jane started rattling her pots and pans again. At last, Sara Lee gobbled down her first brioche in months. Jane started eating her dinners an hour before Alex came home so that an angry though silent protest could be registered. In the course of those early meals, size 12 started pushing toward 14 as the cat munchkin snapped up steak and kidney pie, spinach soufflé, all-natural ice cream with buttered almonds, and more—much more. She had gained a pound and a half and let the mice play in the garden in a spirit of digestive apathy.

It was on a Tuesday that Alex came home from work and found the house dark. Jane had gone to lie down with Sara Lee curled up next to her. The atmosphere was depressing.

"I'm not going to live like this," said Alex in a firm, loud voice. Jane sat up. She been waiting for this. She practically had his bags packed for him.

"No, Jane. We're going to find out what's the matter with us. I like living with you and I won't give that up. Will you try? Let's get some help."

They felt awkward talking to a stranger about their relationship and themselves, but they did it. They did it for several months and held their ground. The Springfields did not become another statistic in the county clerk's office, nor did they allow the lawyers to pick over their bones. The tensions eased and they talked to each other a great deal. There were long discussions and even a little hollering, but they held their ground and made things work.

It was a disaster for Sara Lee. She finally learned to settle for Kitty-Poo and the brown stuff out of the can. By the time she went for her annual checkup, she weighed a chic eight pounds and received thorough approval from her personal physician. It is just another case history, one of many, where a good marriage counselor has saved a cat's life.

———————

A cat living on its own eats because its stomach is empty, the same as any of the larger species of wild cat. However, many domestic cats eat out of habit. Eating patterns are developed with a human partner, and their usefulness is determined by the sensibility of the human setting those patterns.

If a cat is fed by a human with a neurotic relationship with food (or a neurotic relationship with the cat itself), then chances are that the food is given with more purpose than merely filling an empty stomach. With all mammals, food has no further value than the metabolized energy and nutrients provided by it. Human beings, however, too often eat more food than is necessary to sustain life because of an abstract idea of what food means in emotional or psychological terms. Sara Lee's owner ate too much and fed her cat too much because she was unhappy and that's what she did when she was unhappy. For some reason, the act of cooking and eating made her feel more secure, more loved.

When food is presented to house pets with a great deal of emotional fanfare and ballyhoo, and in continuing large quantities, that animal quickly associates the human's emotions as a coded message for feeding. As Pavlov's dogs salivated at the ringing of the dinner bell, so will a domestic cat slurp at the slightest emotional outburst. The cat will respond the way it has been taught to respond. It is unfortunate that most humans fail to realize that their behavior in front of animals (and children) creates responses to that behavior which can be neurotic, destructive, and difficult to change.

Cats wheel and deal with their owners much more than dogs. They are great manipulators and somehow know how to create for themselves the pampered "good life" to perfection. Observing a cat toy with a mouse leads us to conclude that manipulation is the feline's stock in trade. The play behavior of cats and kittens is highly imaginative and demonstrates basic, primitive perceptions such as affecting a pose of indifference prior to pouncing. The cat owner who can resist being manipulated will in the long run have a healthier, more natural pet.

One of the most irksome problems associated with house cats is the obsession for one kind of food over everything else in existence. Once a human hits on the food that the cat seems to prefer, he or she will continue to feed that same old thing for years. The cat will insist on that one thing only and never adjust to a change, even when it might be necessary for medical reasons. Because cats hunt according to the patterned behavior of their various prey they seem to be extremely patterned themselves and rarely deviate from a routine. Any change at all in the cat's routine or home environment is very upsetting to him and requires a very long period of adjustment, if any is possible. Whether it be another animal added to the household, a move to a new residence, or a change to a different brand of cat food, it is not accepted by the cat with grace and good humor. However, this is not a problem that exists in the wild. Quite often wild cats will eat birds, fish, or even insects when there is nothing better on the menu.

Cat owners should understand that felines originated as desert creatures which can survive for long periods of time without food and water. A wild cat will not pass up a chance at a mule deer simply because it prefers the taste of snowshoe rabbit. One should not feed a pet with a French restaurant attitude or emotional pose. This type of behavior serves to distort the animal's natural attitude toward food, that feeding is for the sake of survival.

The accepted expression of affection and love is through stroking, petting, holding, and eye-to-eye verbalizing. Love (or other emotional expressions) by way of food is not only damaging to the cat's natural behavior, it is destructive to the cat's health as well. Eating is the domestic cat's obsession. Such behavior creates serious medical problems. Variety is the key to good feline nutrition. Check the nutrition charts in this chapter for a guide to feeding a balanced diet to a cat.

When a human takes on the responsibility of a pet, its care must be based on the animal's physical and emotional needs rather than the owner's. Overfeeding shortens its life and creates unwarranted illnesses. If you feed your cat commercially prepared food, be certain that the label says it is a complete and balanced diet rather than a snack-type. Inexpensive cat foods are more likely to contain low-quality protein with a high ash and water content, thus offering an inadequate calorie count. By necessity, this type of food forces the owner to overfeed the animal in order to meet the calorie requirements for daily maintenance of growth. However, this does not guarantee full nourishment.

A good diet for your cat is a combination of varied commercial cat foods five days a week, raw organ meat twice a week (for the evening meal), raw egg yolk twice a week (in place of the morning serving of commercial food), and occasional meals of cheese, cooked fish, ground raw beef, cooked vegetables, yogurt, or soups. Give your cat one teaspoonful of corn oil once a day. Vitamin and mineral supplements are a good idea, especially for the lactating or aging cat. Consult your veterinarian. Leave a bowl of water near your cat's food on a twenty-four-hour basis.

Do not feed your cat a diet based exclusively on meat. If you feed your cat fish, be certain it is cooked. This is especially important in the case of freshwater fish. Raw fish will rob the body of some of the B vitamins. Here again, never feed fish exclusively. Raw vegetables are difficult for a cat to digest. Serve them cooked. Dog foods do not meet the nutritional requirements of your cat. Do not be tempted just because you live with both dog and cat. Tomato juice can be very valuable for a cat with chronic cystitis; it will acidify the urine, thus reducing bacterial growth and, in some cases, the formation of crystalline sediment. Do not feed your cat raw egg whites, raw fish, excessive amounts of canned fish, or excessive amounts of liver (raw, cooked, or canned). Use your instincts when it comes to how much is too much.

If your cat is obese or even slightly overweight, turn to the chart, "Daily Food Requirements of Cats According to Age." Determine the proper weight for your pet and what its daily ration should be. You may then reduce your fat cat's diet down to 60 percent of its normal food quantity until enough weight has been lost.

The following charts and tables will further aid in giving your cat the proper diet: caloric requirements and the proper balance of protein, carbohydrates, fat, vitamins, and minerals.

Proper feeding habits and nutritional input are as important to your pet's behavior as training, breeding, and human/pet interaction. As nutrition advances to a sophisticated scientific discipline, its relationship to dog and cat health, both mental and physical, becomes more apparent.

Daily Food Requirements of Cats According to Age

Age	Expected Wt. kg.	Expected Wt. lb.	Daily calorie/body wt. Kcal./kg.	Daily calorie/body wt. Kcal./lb.	Daily ration g.	Daily ration oz.
Newborn	0.12	0.26	380	172	30	1.1
5 weeks	0.5	1.1	250	113	83	2.9
10 weeks	1	2.2	200	91	133	4.7
20 weeks	2	4.4	130	59	173	6.1
30 weeks	3	6.6	100	45	200	7.1
Adult ♂	4.5	9.9	80	36	240	8.5
Adult ♀ (pregnant)	3.5	7.7	100	45	233	8.2
Adult ♀ (lactating)	2.5	5.5	250	113	416	14.7
Neuter ♂	4	8.8	80	36	213	7.5
Neuter ♀	2.5	5.5	80	36	133	4.7

"Ideal" Rations for Cats

	Water %	Protein %	Fat %	Carb. %	Ash %	Calcium %	Kcal./ 100g.
1. Newborn	72	9.5	6.8	10	0.75	0.035	142
2. Kitten & Cats	70	14	10	5	1	0.6	150

Recommended Vitamin Allowances for the Cat

Vitamin	Daily dietary allowance	Comment
A (alcohol or ester)	500–700 µg. (1500–2100 I.U.)	Cannot utilize carotene
D (cholecalciferol)	50–100 I.U.	May synthesize in skin
K (menaquinone)	Negligible	Intestinal synthesis (Probable)
E (alpha-tocopherol)	2–4 mg.	Proportional to polyunsaturated fatty acid content
B_1 (thiamin)	0.2–1 mg. (or 0.1 mg. per 50 kcal. diet)	Increase in lactation or fever
B_2 (riboflavin)	0.15–2 mg.	Increase in lactation or fever and on high fat diet
Niacin (nicotinic acid)	2.6–4 mg.	Increase in lactation or fever; cannot synthesize
B_6 (pyridoxine)	0.2–0.3 mg.	Increase in lactation or fever
Pantothenic acid	0.25–1 mg.	
Biotin	0.1 mg.	
Choline	100 mg.	
Inositol	10 mg.	Essential
B_{12} (cyanocobalamin)	Unknown	Intestinal synthesis (cobalt present)
Folic acid (folacin)	Unknown	Must be present in food
C (ascorbic acid)	Negligible	Metabolic synthesis

Recommended Daily Mineral Allowances for the Cat

Major Mineral Elements	Range	Comments
Sodium	20 to 10 mg.	This is minimum intake
Sodium chloride	1000 to 1500 mg.	Common salt requirement
Potassium	80 to 200 mg.	Adequate in meat and fish
Calcium	200 to 400 mg.	In growth and lactation˙ give 400 mg.
Phosphorus	150 to 400 mg.	Calcium/phosphorus ratio between 0.9 and 1.1 to 1.0
Minor and Trace Elements		
Magnesium	80 to 110 mg.	Usually present in larger amounts
Iron	5 mg.	Iron from hemoglobin is available
Iodine	100 to 400 µg.	Can be deficient in meat
Manganese	200 µg.	
Zinc	250 to 300 µg.	Normally adequate in a
Cobalt	100 to 200 µg.	mixed diet

Feeding a pet dog or cat a proper diet, one that maintains the animal without producing excessive weight gain or loss, is probably the most important kindness a human can give to that pet. Good nutrition promises long life, good health, and a happy relationship.

CHAPTER THREE

A GUIDE FOR HOUSEBREAKERS (Toileting)

Cats

There are two chores in a cat household that make everyone run for cover. One; delivering kittens and two; cleaning the sweet pussycat's litter pan. Grown women have cried and men have been known to throw tantrums over dealing with a cat box. Whether it's a nasty task or just another simple chore depends on your attitude toward the more basic aspects of life.

Taking care of pets has certain similarities to being a parent. Talk to any mother or father who has changed diapers, and you'll hear the full range of attitudes toward the eliminative material that daily departs the mammalian body. The feelings swing from revulsion to toleration to jocularity. It's the same problem with cats. However, dear cat owner, if you do not wish to clean out your kitty's toilet, consider the alternative!

With the notion that it will have a soothing effect to understand the complexity of your cat's eliminative behavior, an explanation is sympathetically offered. If it doesn't help matters, skip this section and turn immediately to the next chapter.

Accepting the premise that the domestic cat is to some degree derivative of the larger species living in the wild it is safe to say that they share many behavioral instincts through genetically organized behavior. With that in mind, consider that the tiger can range between 30 and 600 miles and rarely be detected by its enemies or victims. Part of the reason for its success is its careful habit of burying its urine and feces. In the wild, cats are not particularly anxious to have other animals aware of their exact location within their previously set boundaries. That would give too much of an advantage to a potential meal-on-the-hoof or to a competitor or enemy. It is also important to understand that cats delineate territorial boundaries with their urine and droppings. Once a cat has scent-posted for the sake of territory it then carefully buries all other body eliminations. That means there are two distinct ways cats use their eliminative habits to communicate.

The territory of a cat (both wild and domestic) is not as simple as it might seem. It consists of a network of paths, resting places, sunning spots, and a lair or den (rather than fixed boundaries). The territory is a very limited area that is surrounded by a much greater space called "a range." This, too, is crisscrossed by established paths and is the area in which the animal hunts for food and maintains an outer defense perimeter. Ranges and sometimes home territories of two or more cats will overlap out of necessity, but the overlapping is hardly ever a problem. Two cats with overlapping ranges will do their best to avoid making contact unless it's for mating. Cats seldom defend the outer perimeters of a range, perhaps because they continually move with the migrating herds. Predators must keep up with their prey if they want to eat. We can conclude from this that territory, no matter how well established, is only as important as the wild game that lives on it.

Domesticity is a distorting factor here. Much feline behavior can be difficult to understand when taken out of the context of the genetically organized behavior which no longer serves a purpose. Burying feces, for example, to avoid detection by enemies or scent-posting with feces (or urine) to establish a hunting range and home territory are hardly necessary for the typical domestic cat living in a small apartment in the city. And yet, even this mild-mannered kitty-cat will perform the rituals of the wild. Place that fur-covered homebody in a new territory, and some distant drumbeat from another time sends coded messages and imprinted behavior takes over.

Leon was a true American cat. He was what the Cat Fancy called a silver tabby. To the not-so-fancy, he was a common gray tiger with black stripes—from the genus Alley. Everyone in the neighborhood knew and adored Leon Simpson, *cat ordinaire* from the Simpson residence down the block. Leon had wooed the ladies in the neighborhood just once before his untimely operation, but he had never forgotten that summer in Levittown. Neither had the ladies in the neighborhood. He had won his whiskers.

Marsha Simpson couldn't have been happier with her three-year-old cat. He was affectionate and yet somewhat aloof. He ate with great gusto whatever she spooned out of the can, and he slept soundly every night. Even though he was allowed outdoors during the warm weather, he still used the litter box every day like the neat gentleman he was. He liked the idea that it was placed in the bathroom. During the day Leon always found something to take up his time without intruding on the daily household routine. There was always a bird that needed watching from a safe window or a dog to mock from afar. His great luxury was a delicious stretch and scratch session on his carpeted post that he knew belonged to him alone. It was cat heaven. It was also people's paradise because Leon was about as fine a pet as anyone could ask for.

Leon, Marsha Simpson, and her husband Jerry fell from paradise when they moved from Levittown to Encino, California. They moved because Jerry had been given a transfer with a promotion in his company. On the day the house was emptied by the movers, Leon walked about the echoing hallways and let out a horrible yeeeowp that stirred the marrow of the bones with its awfulness. He let out the same yeeeowp after everything had been moved into the new house in Encino. Leon roamed about sniffing and examining. He was miserable.

During their first week in the new house, the Simpsons were so busy unpacking and trying to decorate that they did not have much time to notice that Leon was not happy. He let out an occasional sound that simulated the Spanish Inquisition, but no one was listening. The problem was that Jerry's boss and wife were invited to dinner in one week as a get-acquainted get-together. The pressure to get the house finished was enormous, and Jerry and Marsha were tense with each other more than a few times.

On a Wednesday afternoon, the doorbell rang, and the next-door neighbor appeared as a welcoming committee of one to introduce herself. The hanging of the draperies came to a stop, and cartons of crockery were moved off the couch as Marjorie Kingman was served a cup of coffee and thanked for her thoughtfulness. Marsha was particularly pleased to meet someone—anyone—from their new neighborhood. While pleasant chitchat was going on, Marjorie watched Leon's movements with fascination as he squatted over a corner of the new decorator-blue all-wool carpet and commenced releasing a half pint of inner liquid.

"Do you realize what your cat is doing?" inquired neighbor Kingman.

Marsha let out a howl and Jerry shouted at Leon, "Stop that!" Poor Leon cringed and then ran out of the room. Marjorie said she had noticed that the house smelled somewhat catty. Upon careful investigation, Marsha and Jerry and the new neighbor discovered that Leon had been using various nooks and crannies around the house for his toilet in addition to his litter.

"Well," said Marjorie, "I'd better let you two settle this." With that she said good-bye, welcome to the neighborhood, and wished them luck with the new house and job.

Leon's indiscretions went on for days, and the Simpsons were going stark raving mad trying to stay one step ahead of him. Their perfect cat had changed into a one-man chamber of horrors. Leon was not happy. Marsha and Jerry were not happy.

"What if Leon decides to let loose while our company is here Saturday?" asked Jerry in terror.

Marsha was worried and thought about it. "Look," she said, "while they're here, we'll just keep the little rat locked in our room." She thought about it and added, "Maybe we'll lock him in the guest room—and cover the furniture with plastic." They need only have looked at the restless, unhappy Leon to know this was a mistake. But desperate circumstances created desperate measures.

Somehow the house was made ready by Saturday night and looked quite charming and cozy. Leon—the rat —who by now was regarded as a saboteur, was placed in the guest room with his food and water bowls behind a firmly closed door. The doorbell rang, and Jerry said with sarcasm, "Let the games begin!"

Ruth and James McCann were affable, warm, and amusing. They were ideal guests. Much to their surprise, Marsha and Jerry had a very pleasant evening getting acquainted with the head of the branch office. There was much discussion about the virtues and headaches of

Southern California, golf, shopping, tennis, the price of coffee, where Johnny Carson really lived, and more. Long after dinner—a very fine dinner—Ruth McCann said she thought she heard a strange sound. Nobody else heard it, and the after-dinner talk continued to roll along. Then everyone heard something. Yep. It was a very distant YEEEOWP!

"That's a cat," proclaimed Ruth. "There isn't much I don't know about cats, and that's a cat," said the concerned Mrs. McCann, who forced her tolerant husband to live with six of them.

First Jerry and then Marsha explained to the very interested woman the problem they were having with good old Leon. "To avoid embarrassment," concluded Marsha, "we shut Leon away in the guest room so that he wouldn't turn the evening into a disaster."

Ruth McCann walked to the guest room, saying, "Well, that won't help anything. You're just upsetting the cat more than he already is from the move. He needs to be convinced that he's safe. Bring the pussycat to me. I'll take care of him." Marsha raced her to the door and opened it. Leon darted out immediately into the outstretched arms of Mrs. McCann, who scooped him up and brought him out into the living room.

The guest room had been dark, so Leon had trouble adjusting his eyes to the brightly lit living room. Ruth returned to her comfortable armchair and began petting and stroking Leon as she continued the original conversation. Once the pleasant talk began again, nobody took notice of the contented Leon who sat on the soft, short lap like a sphinx at a massage parlor. His eyes were closed and he looked as though he were trying to remember something important.

The rest of the evening passed quickly, and Ruth shushed everyone. She pointed down at the cat on her lap and whispered, "He's asleep. Look, Marsha, if you simply hold this cat for a while each day he'll settle down and stop being such a swine. He needs loving reassurance from both of you, and then he'll go back to his sweet self again."

Mr. McCann got up and headed for the guest room. Jerry asked why he was going there, and McCann answered, "To get our coats and my hat. I put them there when we first arrived."

Jerry tried to hide the worry from his face and Marsha held her breath as they waited for McCann to return to the living room. From down the hall they heard him groan, "Oh, no! My hat. Not my hat!"

———◆———

There may be no animal more concerned with territory than the domestic cat. It is difficult for a wild cat to survive without a range in which to hunt for food. Sharing the prey with a competitor is totally unacceptable to the solitary predator. The domestic cat suffers from this territorial hangover even though its survival is not at stake. If you remove a domestic cat from its established home territory and hunting range, be prepared to deal with an emotionally upset animal. In addition, the cat's sense of security is derived from well-established patterns of behavior. In the wild, these patterns can be so entrenched as to enable a cat to walk in its own previously made footprints along well-established paths. When a drastic change is initiated, such as a move from one house to another, the animal becomes emotionally stressed. One of the manifestations of the stress is a refusal to use the litter box, exclusively. Your pet may become obsessed with creating scent posts along the outer perimeters of the new home range. Most cats seem much more concerned with *where* they live than *with whom* they live.

During such a period of transition, your cat must be given a great deal of reassurance and extra attention. The animal must not be allowed outdoors for a while to prevent it from running away in an uncontrollable attempt to return to the original territory. Although not practiced by every cat, running away is a genetically organized impulse to recover lost territory. Cougars, leopards, and other wild cats never leave their range unless their prey migrates. There have been countless stories of cats traveling hundreds—indeed, thousands of miles to return to a former owner that abandoned the animal. The question is whether the animal was returning to *someone* or *someplace.*

When marking off new territory, it is desirable from the cat's perspective to leave his scent on some vertical object off the ground. In the wild, a tree or bush is usually selected. This is instinctive behavior, and it may be for the purpose of attracting a mate or warning the competition. This marking is accomplished with an odorous urine that is easier for other cats to discern from off the ground. The cat backs up against the object and urinates or defecates on it in a backward, quivering motion. It is quite possible that a cat will select the wall or door or chair leg in a new home for scent-posting and do its best (or worst) to claim the new territory. In the wild, a cat also follows this scent posting action with a claw marking to show his height to the other members of the cat society. Forewarned is forearmed.

Housebreaking Your Cat

Most cats and kittens arrive in their new homes as trained ladies and gentlemen who have been taught toilet manners by their mothers. However, there are those who have not had enough time with their mothers to know what it's all about. Nothing could be easier than house training a cat. It is important to understand that cats have an emotional need to quickly develop a toilet area that allows them to bury their wastes.

A cat's emotional and physical state is revealed in its toilet behavior. When it is in poor health or emotionally upset, it fails to use its established toilet area. If this were to happen in the wild the cat's location would be revealed, which would place the animal in grave danger. When domestic cats fail to follow the dictates of house training, they are either sick or disturbed and must be dealt with on that level rather than summarily punished.

There has been too much emphasis of late on the "emotions" of house pets, with a strong implication that those emotions are identical to human feelings based on human needs. If this were true, there should have been an uprising by now of all pet dogs and cats. There would certainly be some form of emancipation movement to rid themselves of the leashes, collar, cages, pens, kennels, and chains of restraint. If pets have human emotions, then they must share that one driving desire of *Homo sapiens:* to be free, independent, and self-reliant.

Because there is no longer a large, wild frontier in which to release our pet population, they must live as they do in human society, and that defines itself as a benevolent dictatorship between human and animal. The pet is totally dependent and the human is extremely needful. The animal needs a full belly and the human craves companionship, no questions asked. It's a fair exchange between the two.

No one has yet been able to prove that animals experience or behave with such sophisticated human emotions as spite, revenge, resentment, guilt, despair, contempt, modesty, or bashfulness. With almost no exception, these emotions in dogs and cats are more accurately termed "fear" and can be cataloged as variations and degrees of fear. Animals do not have vices or virtues as defined by a human morality system. They behave in response to their immediate needs.

Pets do not relieve themselves on their owners' beds as an act of defiant spitework, but rather because something frightens them—perhaps being left alone. Certainly animals have emotions, but they are more basic than those described above. They form attachments to humans and to other animals, and we could arbitrarily call it love. They also experience anger, disgust, impatience, surprise, etc. but only in the immediate sense. They do not mull over things that make them angry or brood about the injustice of the world. Animals have egos, but only in the existential sense. Dogs and cats (the healthy ones) have a form of egotism that makes them continually refer to themselves in all situations. Like human babies, it is the only way they know they exist.

Cats do not go off their house training to spite or upset their owners. It is because they are sick (the most common ailment is a bladder infection which causes a urinary blockage), disturbed over the loss of a companion animal or human, or because their environment has been tampered with or changed in some way. With these exceptions, cats can be easily housebroken and expected to remain clean and well trained. It is what they prefer.

Obviously, a litter box or pan is needed. These are readily available in all pet-supply shops and in many supermarkets. They are made of plastic or hard rubber, and you can buy disposable plastic liners to facilitate cleaning. There are cardboard litter boxes that are completely disposable, and some people even use empty beer-bottle cartons, which are small and shallow, like a litter pan. The most common substance to go in the pan is granulated clay, which is sold in most markets as kitty litter. Sand is efficient, as is sawdust or soil from your backyard.

The location of the cat's toilet is, of course, a matter of personal preference. In small apartments it is usually put in the bathroom. There are cat pans now available that are completely covered, with only a small portal for the cat to go in and out of. This affords the cat privacy and its humans a sense of delicacy about the whole affair. In a full-size house, the basement, garage or back pantry are where the pan is usually placed.

It is important to your cat's training to confine him to the house and not let him out until you are certain he understands using the litter pan. With few exceptions, all cats have a need to eliminate immediately following a meal or a drink of water. A vigorous play period will also induce your cat to relieve himself. At those times, carry your cat to the litter pan and place him inside. Hold his front paws and move them back and forth in the clay. You are actually teaching the cat to scratch in the sandy substance. This activity is very pleasant for the cat—at least it is compelling. Here you are merely showing him a place to dig and bury his body waste. Now inherited behavior takes over. This behavior should instigate the cat's desire to eliminate, and once he does you are just about home free. Repeat this action several times if your cat does not respond properly. Patience and persistence are the keys to training all animals. Do not forget to confine your cat to the house and, if you can stand it, to the room in which the pan is located, until the training is complete. When he eliminates outdoors, it becomes harder to teach the use of the litter pan, and that can become very inconvenient.

Once your cat is using the pan, do not relocate it in some other part of the house or apartment. The same is true for the kind of litter you place inside. Remember, cats do not adjust to changes very well and may lose their house training for a while if something isn't right. It is also necessary to maintain a clean box, or the fastidious dears will not touch it. To the cat's sensibility, a dirty, smelly litter pan reveals its presence to its enemies and violates its instinct for survival. Clean the cat box every day!

Cats goof their training when they are not well. The most common problem is a urinary blockage caused by cystitis. In an effort to pass urine, the cat will piddle small quantities in many different parts of the house. Call your veterinarian immediately—your cat's life is in serious danger.

Altered male and female cats are good candidates for consistent house training. Among the many benefits of spaying and castrating is that your cat will be a perfectly house-trained animal and will use the litter pan exclusively (except when ill). A cat in good health eating a well-balanced diet should remain a joy forever and experience the sweet smell of success.

Dogs

"Housebreaking" is one of those words like "prunes"—it always gets a laugh, or at least a silly smirk. Housebreaking never gets a laugh from a novice dog owner with a seven-month-old Alaskan malamute who leaves calling cards all over the house. Housebreaking also gets few laughs from the owner of the toy dog who dumps in the middle of the bed at the Holiday Inn.

Like pregnancy, a dog is never partially housebroken. "In for a dime in for a dollar." It is of no use to a dog owner to have an animal reliable for seven days in a row and then have to step in something left behind on the eighth. Unless the animal is sick, there is no reason to tolerate an unhousebroken dog.

From your dog's point of view, the elimination of body waste is just about the least important reason to urinate and defecate. These functions comprise the most effective means of communication (with other dogs, primarily) nature has provided. Although a dog possesses keen vision, his sense of smell is even better. When one dog urinates or defecates in a particular locale, sooner or later all other dogs in the area become aware of it no matter how long the material has been sitting there. A dog's nose is his most efficient mechanism. He can smell better than humans and can discern and file away in his memory over ten thousand separate and distinct odors.

Dogs proclaim for all others in the area, "I am here" whenever they eliminate in a city street or on a country bush. Sometimes it is an effort to communicate with their human family if they are lost. In the wild, territory is marked off with this scent-posting technique, and members of the same pack know the parameters of their pack's terrain. It is also a warning to members of other packs that this area is spoken for and is a guide to proper pack identification. The hunting range for wolves changes with the migration of prey animals and is determined in part by weather conditions and food availability. Therefore, scent-posting is a continuing activity as the pack moves from terrain to terrain.

We must view the domestic dog's eliminative behavior with this in mind. Just like wolves, pet dogs continue to mark their imagined territory with urine and droppings. They no longer know why they do it, but some vestigial wire continues to function in an abandoned printed circuit in the lost passageways of the brain. Like a message in a bottle or light traveling from a star, a dog's eliminations send out personal information to others passing through his time and space.

Sex is another important factor involved in the elimination of urine and fecal matter. When a female is in heat, she produces a strong odor that is present in the waste matter. It is yet another technique of communicating the fact that a female in the territory is in season and ready to mate. Male dogs are magnetically drawn to this odor and attempt to find nature's temptress. When it comes to housebreaking problems for dog owners, there is more to it than meets the eye.

Harold Greer gave his wife Doris a Yorkshire terrier puppy for her twenty-eighth birthday. He had gone to a great deal of trouble, and he made the purchase with the help of a list of breeders supplied by the American Kennel Club. Doris cooed with pleasure as she clutched the tiny canine and in an instant named him Pudding. He peed all over her blouse.

Newspapers were spread out on a portion of the

kitchen floor and all manner of sign language and primitive grunts were tried in order to communicate what they wanted from the small dog. It was always too late by the time the papers were spread out. They'd place the small animal on the Sunday magazine and tell Pudding to wee-wee, to pee-pee, to make, to go, to give mommy her jewels, to let it all hang out, to make plop-plops, to move, to try, to crappy and, finally, to drop dead. To their complete and utter frustration, Pudding always seemed to wait until he was allowed into the living room before letting loose.

Mr. Greer sold diamonds at Cartier's and was accustomed to a muted, dignified existence. But even this subdued gentleman lost his composure and began quietly stepping on Pudding's paws behind Mrs. Greer's back. It was clearly an act of retaliation. He once raised his hand to slap the misbehaving dog, but his wife shrieked in horror. His flattened hand turned knuckle-white and throbbed as it sought a place to hide. In the beginning, the little dog eagerly waited for his owners to see his little beads of waste matter and to receive their applause. It soon became apparent that these people did not appreciate his minor triumphs. It was beyond his comprehension. They would yell and holler at his proud little puddles, and all he could do was cock his head to one side and try to read their lips.

Pudding did not read, write, or speak English. Nor did he fathom the peculiar attitude of humans toward fecal declarations of the existential self. His communiqués in dog language were as effective as Western Union and every bit as eloquent as the Hallmark product. What was wrong? He was in a foreign country on a raincheck and was trying very hard to become streetwise, but no one knew how or what to teach him. And so, every once in a while, he knew he was going to be yelled at and punished in some way. He resigned himself to the daily unpleasantness of being a prisoner of war.

Through a process of trial and error, Pudding learned that they became less upset when he eliminated on their newspapers and absolutely ecstatic when he let go outdoors. But there was nothing definitive about the situation. The dog still found himself compelled to return to the old soiled spots on the carpet and reaffirm his presence with a declaration of assertion written in urine. It did not win him any popularity contests. From the Greers' point of view, the dog was slowly learning how to behave, possibly through osmosis or some feat of extrasensory perception. Doris Greer was convinced that things were going well (a relative term in this case) because she had changed her mantra from Vishnu to Pudding.

Harold Greer was forced to give up his meditation because that was the time the dog chose to relieve himself —a sort of meditation break, as it were. The thought that Pudding was dirtying the wall-to-wall kept creeping into the eastern silence and had the opposite effect of meditation. Greer's response was far from relaxed. His legs would become prickly and restless as if the blood ceased to flow to them. They tingled like sour pickles and his palms would sweat. He hated it when his palms sweated. It reminded him of those awful moments in the upstairs salon just before an important client decided to take or leave a major purchase. Meditation was supposed to make him forget the jewelry business, but Pudding's nutritional residue began to look like necklaces and bracelets.

For days Greer tried hard to accomplish his quiet time, but he always quit early because the dog's face constantly appeared before his closed eyes like a recurring daydream. On the last day he meditated, he valiantly fought the mental picture of Pudding's mess with the word *Ahimsa*, a $100 mantra bought new. His stomach muscles tensed and beads of perspiration formed everywhere as he repeated the word over and over again. Like a child's punishment on the blackboard, he repeated the mantra quickly, then slowly, then faster and faster. By the eighth minute, foam formed at the corners of his mouth, and he was saying the word furiously until he could hear his voice ring against the walls, "AHIMSA, GOD DAMN IT!"

Mr. Greer gave up meditation about the same time that Mrs. Greer decided Pudding was housebroken because he occasionally used the newspapers. Of course that didn't change the dog's love for the carpet. He still kept his hand in, so to speak.

For several months everybody settled for the status quo. Mrs. Greer continued to refer to Pudding as a housebroken dog, and Mr. Greer spent more time at work than ever before. He often came home after his wife had retired for the evening, and he would slip carefully into the dimly lit apartment for fear of stepping on one of Pudding's quasi-housebroken manifestations. This caution was created by an unfortunate incident one evening when he came home and smeared his black patent shoes and the cuff of his gray pinstriped suit. Playing their parts, Doris pretended she was satisfied with the dog's behavior, and Harold discreetly cleaned up. Something good did come out of all this, however. Because of his long hours of overtime spent at the store which was interpreted as devotion to the firm, Cartier, Incorporated promoted Mr. Greer from engagement rings to evening jewelry. The cost of each transaction was breathtaking, and there seemed to be more dignity in dealing with lovers than suitors. It was a seller's market and an exclusive education in the law of supply and demand. It was a step up, he imagined.

The pretense over Pudding came to an abrupt ending during a shocking session in the divorce court. It seemed that from time to time Mr. Greer dipped his hand into more than the velvet necklace trays at work. He was discovered at an intimate restaurant in the company of a frequent client. Doris was passing by the neighborhood bistro and spotted Harold through the window as he was spooning out some chocolate mousse onto the plate of a mascara-eyed, stiff-sprayed blonde not quite past her prime. Doris was walking the dog who stopped directly in front of that fateful window.

Harold stuck by his story. He was working late that evening and wasn't anywhere near a restaurant. She must have mistaken him for someone else. The story didn't wash because he could not explain a dried dollop of chocolate mousse on the cuff of his jacket, his shirtsleeve, and his opal-studded cufflink.

The evidence revealed the truth, and it proved to be an open-and-shut case. All that was left was the fight over alimony and a property settlement. It wound up as a con-tested divorce in court. At the trial, each attorney handed the judge a list of property demands. With more than a little surprise, the judge noted that each had awarded *the other* custody of Pudding. The judge demanded to see the little dog in question and settled the matter by making Pudding a ward of the state. Off the record, the judge summarily adopted the Yorkie, took him home, and house-broke the dog himself according to the advice given in a dog-training manual.

Many months before their final decree, Harold and Doris reconciled their differences. Harold moved back into the apartment after successfully courting his wife. They lived happily ever after—with a cat.

———————

Not everyone should own a dog. And there is no such thing as a half-housebroken dog! Either he is or he isn't. When it comes to body waste, communication is the name of the game. If the animal is not scent-posting, he is telling you something else. For example, a dog's inability to be housebroken is often a barometer of his physical or emotional well-being. A very small breed such as a Yorkshire terrier may be nervous or excitable and have a more difficult time gaining control of his bladder. Excessive wetting can also be a display of submissiveness if your dog is overwhelmed by his family or has been relegated to a subordinate position in his litter.

If a young dog or puppy has worms, and most of them get worms sooner or later, he will not be able to control his body waste. A frightened, bored, lonely, or highly nervous dog has more trouble than a dog on an even emotional keel. There is no such thing as spite in matters pertaining to housebreaking. A dog may eliminate indoors even though he is supposed to be trained not to, but it is never because of spite. To punish or spite a human is simply too sophisticated for a dog.

Sometimes the dog's indoor messing is neurotic, but not in the sense that we understand the word. Here the word "neurotic" means that which is abnormal for dog behavior, such as dirtying his own nest (living area). If a dog messes on his owner's bed, it may be a distress signal or an urgent need to scent-post. It is impossible for this to be a means of punishing a human for leaving the dog alone. Neurotic behavior in dogs is based on fear such as the fear of punishment, thunder, or being left alone. When a dog behaves neurotically, try to understand what it is that he is afraid of and change the conditions of his environment which frighten him. If this is not practical, get help from a professional dog trainer.

It is quite natural for a dog to eliminate in his own territory. Nature has set it up that way. To force a dog not to do it is to go against his nature. What is required is a means of communication to the dog that some behavior displeases you while other behavior pleases you very much. It is counterproductive to attempt to alter your dog's behavior. What is useful is to attempt to alter his environment so that his natural behavior coincides with your needs. In the matter of housebreaking, it is simply a question of extending the animal's territory to the outdoors so that he may stake his claim there instead of on your carpet.

How to Housebreak Your Dog

(1) Select a place outdoors as the toilet ground. Use this locale consistently. (2) Until the dog is housebroken, confine his movements in the house to one room. If he is allowed out of the restricted area, watch him at all times. (3) Take the dog to the toilet area first thing in the morning and last thing in the evening, after each meal, after drinking water, after a nap, after a vigorous play or exercise period. (4) Praise the dog immediately after he relieves himself, outdoors and at the toilet area. (5) Bring him indoors immediately after toileting. Do not let him misinterpret the outing as a play period. (6) Take your dog outside when he gives signals for eliminating such as sniffing the ground or turning in circles. (7) Feed your dog on a consistent schedule so that his need to eliminate will also be on a consistent schedule. If you plan to put him on a self-feeding program, do not start it until he is housebroken. (8) Do not punish the dog if he has an accident. If you catch him in the act, say "No!" in a harsh voice and rush him outdoors to his toilet location. P.S.: Keep a bottle of Nilotex around for urine stains and Airwick's Carpet Fresh as a rug and room deodorizer.

CHAPTER FOUR

THE HEALTH CLUB

Cats

Two sets of tennis, a steam, a rub, and a hot shower would just about turn any cat into a Thanksgiving centerpiece with pink paper panties on the drumsticks. No, the health needs of the family *Felidae* are much different from the needs of the *Homo sapiens*—or are they?

Cats require a clean environment to maintain a germ-free condition. So do humans. Cats must maintain some form of muscle tone so that fat does not interfere with the blood's transportation of oxygen and nutrients to the living cells. The same applies to humans. Cats are obsessed with a sense of personal hygiene through a self-grooming or preening behavior although no one understands why. With some qualifications, the same can be said for humans. Self-grooming and certain forms of social grooming are behavioral traits that all mammals seem to share in one respect or another. That would tend to make all of us members of the same health club—except for the handful of mammalian *shtunks* who wait to be pushed into a bathtub.

Herbie was a dirty cat. It didn't matter much because his owner was pretty much the same. He wasn't very much like other cats in that he never bathed himself unless he was covering up embarrassment or pain. On occasion, Herbie would leap from the floor to a tabletop and miss. Licking his coat in those instances was a deceptive ploy so that you could never tune into his inner monologue which might have been saying, "God damn meeow, that hurts."

He was part Maine coon cat and part feather-duster, a geneticist's bad joke. His fur was always matted in spots, and the occasional white patches on his legs and tail were dirt-gray. It was not usual for a cat to maintain himself in such a poor state of personal hygiene, but Herbie's master was a bad influence on him right from the beginning of their relationship. He lived with Sonny Murn, an importer of tropical fish. Murn had found Herbie when he was one week old, eyes not opened yet, abandoned and almost dead. With the help of baby formula fed through the fingers of a rubber glove, the thrown-away kitten survived. On the twelfth day of his life, when his eyes opened, the first thing on earth that he saw was a large, hairy beast that was as unkempt and disheveled a creature as he would ever find.

Murn was forty-one and was serving a life sentence in the same factory loft in which he conducted his tropical fish hatchery and importing business. He lived alone by choice—his and everyone else's.

Murn's quarters bubbled and gurgled twenty-four hours a day with tanks of green-blue water. There were four hundred metal-framed aquariums in his loft, set in eight even rows like columns of obedient deep-sea divers marching to Victor Herbert's music. The aquariums held twenty, forty, sixty, or one hundred gallons each with their glass coastlines slapped by thousands of valuable tropical fish. The loft had special heat pipes running horizontally against the wall in parallel, helping to maintain a warm environment for the South American immigrants. The individual tanks were kept warm with glass tubular heaters immersed directly in the water. It was a hot, brilliantly colored sight in Sonny Murn's loft, and it was home for a dirty cat named Herbie.

Although Herbie had been well treated all of his life, he was not exactly pampered as a kitten. Sonny was not an overly affectionate soul, and only on rare occasions gave him a sweaty-palmed pat on the head. Still, both man and cat understood each other quite well, and each respected the other's wishes and limitations.

Now, one would think that a fishery would be cat heaven for a dingy little vagabond like Herbie, but it wasn't. In the beginning of his career, as a tropical-fish cat, he made the mistake of sticking his paw in a tank with several mean little monsters from South America. As Herbie tried to scoop out a deceptively docile fish, it unexpectedly bit his dewclaw and damn near pulled him in. Herbie lost a bit of tissue and bled for hours. He did not go near the tanks again. But he was a sucker for those tasty little neon tetras with their iridescent blue stripes and red tails. On occasion, Sonny would deliberately drop one or two to the floor so that Herbie could have a pleasant pounce. But Herbie had learned his lesson and never stuck his paw in an aquarium again. He was satisfied with catching the spill.

Watching Sonny asleep on his one stuffed chair near the window overlooking the street, with Herbie flat out on his lap, was quite a sight. They looked like father and cat, both with unkempt hair, dull complexions, broken moustache whiskers growing out in peculiar whichway directions. Sonny had longish fingernails that showed the dirt from his daily labors. Herbie's nails were also long and dirty.

Although Sonny spent only one year in college, he was considered by many to be one of the foremost ichthyologists in the country. He received mail from people all over the world seeking information about this species or that and of course it contributed to the success of his business. Insulated cartons of tropical fish were constantly arriving or leaving the huge loft, and because the eccentric man worked alone, he did all of the loading and unloading. For that reason he and his cat napped whenever they could find a spare minute. Merchandising ichthyology was tough enough for a human, but it was absolutely grueling for a cat.

One Thursday afternoon, arriving with a carton of *Pterophyllum eimekei* (angelfish) from the Amazon, was a woman in a khaki skirt and jacket. She was over thirty and had brown hair and blue eyes.

"Dr. Murn, I presume?" she mused.

"Huh?"

"You are Dr. Eustace T. Murn, aren't you?"

"I'm Murn. I sell fish."

"I'm Cornelia Horton. From Borja . . . Brazil. I wrote to you about the angelfish."

"Oh my God! What are you doing here?" asked Sonny, overcome with amazement.

"Well, my father died last month, and I've come home to the States. Of course, I've never been here, but as far as I'm concerned, it's always been home. Actually, you're the only person I know in this country, so here I am."

Sonny had been answering Cornelia Horton's correspondence for seven years and had been explaining the pains and pleasures of ichthyology. But he did that with dozens of correspondents around the world. He never expected to actually meet one. As the woman marched up the stairs into his life the disheveled fish man made a feeble gesture of brushing his hair with his palm. His hands dangled as he followed her up. Dirty Herbie remained on the sidewalk. He was suspicious.

Within five days, Sonny Murn's eggs were fried, his pants were washed, and his fingernails were trimmed and cleaned for his wedding. The next day Cornelia and Sonny became a family as the two enjoyed a brief honeymoon at the Coney Island Aquarium and watched the feeding of the whales. On the seventh day they rested . . . until eight in the morning.

"And now," said Cornelia ominously, "this place."

"What's the matter with this place?" demanded Sonny, digging a deeper hole in the mattress.

"I'll tell you what's the matter with it. It's filthy. It's not fit for human habitation. A troop of gorillas would pass it by. We're going to clean it all."

"All?" he groaned.

"All," she snapped as she pulled his blanket off the bed. For ten hours Mr. and Mrs. Murn swept, mopped, dusted, polished, put away, threw out, bagged in plastic, scoured, boiled, and carted. Despite all its aquariums and cartons of supplies, the loft began to take on a scrubbed neatness. The wooden floors glistened like a maindeck, and the walls were whitewash clean. With all the blazing colors of the tropical fish swimming in green-blue the place surfaced with a spartan stylishness indicative of the Soho district with its artists' quarters and galleries.

"Well, it's finished. I hope you're happy," said Sonny as he wiped his brow.

"Not quite."

"For God's sake, you cleaned everything including the air hoses and light chains. What more do you want?"

Cornelia squinted her eyes, and with her hands on her hips, answered, "I want that Herbie."

"Wait a minute," glared Sonny. "I've accepted the whole package here, but I'm not going to let you make that cat miserable." The two of them plopped down, ex-

hausted, in hard folding chairs, watched by thousands of
bulging eyes from the tanks. All that could be heard were
the bubbles. After many minutes, Cornelia was the first to
break the silence.

"Can you explain to me why cleaning the filthy beast
would make him miserable?"

Sonny cleared his throat and answered. "The cat lives
on his own—in and out of the loft. He's part street cat. A
tough guy. I make no demands and neither does he. He's a
natural sort of a cat, and you've no right to make him
change. It would be a betrayal. He's got rights. And so do
I, and that's where I draw the line. Forget it!"

Cornelia was very quiet during and after Sonny's
speech. She was moved by what he said and sighed
deeply. "I understand what you feel, and I apologize.
Please forgive me for what I've done. I'm afraid it's too
late." She rose from her chair and walked to the bathroom
door and opened it.

"Okay, Herbie. You can come out now."

Stepping into the room was a half Maine coon cat half
mink stole, sparkling with clean, shiny fur. He had been
bathed, brushed, powdered, clipped, and slicked down.
There was a wide red ribbon tied into a bow around his
neck. Sonny stared at the old boy. He wanted to burst into
laughter but didn't for the old times' sake. He simply shook
his head from side to side, got up, and went to work feeding his fish. With the tension broken, Cornelia went to the
other side of the room and began feeding the fish in the
opposite banks of aquariums. The fish were fed in silence
as Herbie sat in the middle of the floor not sure what to do
next. Sonny dipped his net into the neon tetras' tank and
flicked three of them onto the floor. Herbie pounced on
them and gulped them down in three seconds. Somehow,
though, it just wasn't the same. So he removed the red
ribbon in one swipe, stepped onto the fire escape, and disappeared over the rooftops. He did not return. It boiled

down to the fact that Sonny could change and Herbie could not.

Sonny grieved and tried not to look at Cornelia with resentment. He couldn't know the good time that Herbie was having. He had moved into an Italian fish store and proven his worth as a mouser before he was discovered. Who could deny a job to a good mouser? And so, dirty Herbie waited for each day to end and get his matted paws into the fish cleaner's can. It was the most disgusting cat heaven there was. Now and then Herbie showed up on the fire escape and looked in on Sonny and Cornelia. They were very happy to see him and showed it, each in their way. Cornelia would give the cat a thorough scrubbing and Sonny would give him a crack at some neon tetras. It was . . . an arrangement.

Normally, a dull coat and listlessness indicate that a cat is sick or about to get sick. It is rare that a healthy cat will not preen itself by licking its coat. However, there are cases such as Herbie the Dirty Cat where the animal has been influenced in a very specific life-style and finds it difficult if not impossible to change. Even though alley cats make grooming efforts, it is useless. They are a mess minutes after cleaning themselves.

For people who attend cat shows and are intrigued with the Cat Fancy, grooming is an aesthetic factor. Much is made of various shampoos and coat conditioners, brushes, combs, and nail clippers. They are all valid and wonderful for the cat. But one must consider grooming from a health point of view first and a beauty treatment second.

At the very least, dirt on a cat's body will cause a variety of skin ailments which can become serious. Bear in mind that whatever is in or on the cat's fur will eventually be ingested in the body by the licking technique used in self-grooming. A cat may ingest anything from parasites to broken glass. Fleas, ticks, lice, and worms carry with them infection and potentially fatal illnesses.

For these reasons a cat should be brushed every day, combed once a week (especially long-haired cats), and bathed about once a month with a high-quality shampoo designed for felines. The skin beneath the fur should be inspected when being groomed and checked for lumps, cuts or skin lesions. An indoor cat's nails may be clipped once a week and inspected between the toes for fleas and other parasites. When a substance such as paint or glue hardens a patch of fur, it is important to remove it as soon as possible. Otherwise the cat will lick at it excessively and ingest more than the normal amount of hair follicles and possibly develop furballs along the digestive tract. These hair formations sometimes cause serious obstructions or unpleasant vomiting. On rare occasions surgery becomes necessary for their removal. Remove hard fur mats by snipping them out with a scissors rather than using kerosene, paint remover, and other petroleum distillate products.

Your cat's ears should be inspected for wax accumulation and wiped out with a damp cloth dipped in mineral oil or water if necessary. This will prevent ear infection. Cleaning the corners of your cat's eyes as solid material develops is also a health-saving practice. Use a soft cloth, lightly dampened. Wrap a section of the cloth around your index finger and gently remove the caked material.

There is no scientific evidence to prove that cats want very much to be clean and smart looking, but there isn't a cat owner in the world who won't say this is true.

Clean means something different to a cat than it means to a human. It is not next to godliness from the cat's point of view. Clean means efficiency and self-preservation. In the wild, self-grooming accomplishes the removal of dead hair from the coat, eliminates the scent from a fresh kill, removes burrs and other irritants (especially from between the toes), and possibly removes its own odor while stalking prey. This must not be confused with the act of getting cleaned by another cat. When one cat grooms another, there is more involved than bathing. There is probably some dominant/ subordinate role playing when cats engage in mutual grooming. It is a parental function to lick kittens clean starting from the moment of birth (in the removal of the amniotic sac) to the stimulation of the infant cat's eliminative system. There can be no doubt that mutual grooming plays some role in social communication between cats, as well.

When a cat does not groom itself, it is either sick or unluckily burdened with an important lack of education. For most cats survival demands personal hygiene and grooming. If you begin grooming your cat in kittenhood, it will make the job easy and tolerable to the animal. Besides brushing, cleaning ears, combing, etc., his or her nails should be trimmed. Purchase a specially designed nail trimmer for cats and use it once a month or when your cat's claws are overly long and sharp. First, place the paw in the palm of your hand. Next, squeeze the pad with your index finger and the top of the toe to be trimmed with your thumb. The nail will appear. Cut the nail just before you see the pinkish color of the quick. Cutting beyond this point will be painful to the animal. To be safe do not cut past the curvature of the claw.

Your cat's teeth should also be cleaned. Once a week is not excessive. Moisten a gauze pad or clean washcloth and scrub the outer surfaces of the teeth and gums. If they bleed, it indicates the beginning of gum disease, and you should consult a veterinarian.

People who live with cats believe that their pets' personal appearance and hygiene make them feel good and somewhat aloof. Cats are creatures of rare dignity and must be permitted this important indulgence. It's only human.

Dogs

A paunchy pooch with sagging shoulders and dragging tail can be a victim of urban blight like any other dweller in the cities of America. The stresses and strains of modern living have their bad effect on dogs as they do on humans. Overcrowding, violence, the exigencies of economic strain, noise, dirt, and supersonic change cause headaches, nervous breakdowns, and death at the higher end of the scale, and listlessness, overweight, and physical deterioration at the lower end. Modern dogs, like modern humans, must take better care of themselves or suffer the consequences. Of course, dogs need more help than humans in this respect. You'll never get a dog to count calories or meditate on his own. And you can forget the daily regimen of the Royal Canadian Air Force Exercises. Dogs are just not self-starters. Those living the good life, all fat and sassy, never think about that great resort in the sky where existence is less than a TV dog-food commercial. Dogs of America! Shape up! Dogs and their owners must learn to relax, to eat sensibly and to get out there and do some exercise.

A young woman fell from her high perch into the ravine and sank down into the fast-rushing stream of water. The large Saint Bernard heard her cry for help while lying on its side, still dazed from being clubbed on the head by the dope smuggler in the checkered shirt. The noble dog somehow staggered to his feet and made a start for the edge of the cliff. He was confronted by a mean-looking rottweiler. The villainous dog snarled, but the Saint Bernard growled such a menacing sound from deep within the throat that the black and tan rottweiler backed away, turned and ran. With that chore settled, he cautiously went to the edge and looked down from the height. He could see his mistress trying to stay above the water as she flailed about. With the determined look of a hero, the dog stood at the edge and poised for the long plunge downward.

"Cut. That's a take," yelled the director. "Set up for shot 215, the dive. Get the stunt dog in makeup."

Mortimer was probably the most beautiful Saint Bernard in the country; at least his millions of fans thought so. The large, noble dog was a film and TV star of great magnitude. He was more than a film star. He was an industry unto himself with Mortimer T-shirts, bubble-gum cards, wristwatches, and board games. The great dog was seen on billboards across the nation and on countless TV commercials selling everything from mutual funds to feminine sprays. The most popular breakfast cereal ran continuing stories of his exploits on the back of the boxes, and charities and businesses competed fiercely for his endorsement.

Mortimer's coat was dazzling in its orange-red and white colors, with black fur around the eyes and ear tops which hung down like velvet flaps. His tail was a brilliant splash of red and white that made his fans scream whenever he waved it in their faces. The Saint Bernard was the star attraction wherever he went. He was seven years old, but the studio publicists claimed he was five. They also planted items in the papers about Mortimer's being something of a ladies' dog, what with a fling with a lovely Afghan here and a borzoi there. The truth of the matter is that the handsome brute suffered from cryptorchidism (a congenital condition in which the testicles have not descended; such dogs are usually sterile) and could never qualify for an American Kennel Club show competition. Uneasy lies the head that wears a crown.

Because Mortimer's fame was so great, his worth to his owner and movie studio was in the millions of dollars. Consequently, they never took chances with his well-being. Despite the fact that his fame was based on heroic exploits, they never allowed him to actually perform the daring deeds. Contagion Filmway Studios had insured him for $15,000,000, and the policy stipulated that all actions involving potentially hazardous consequences to life and limb had to be performed by other dogs. So the studio purchased a stable of Saint Bernard stunt dogs who, though valuable themselves, never came close to the star's value.

Mortimer began life in an exclusive kennel with parents who were AKC Champions of Record. Because of the puppy's splendid conformation, it was assumed that he would make a great show dog. As he got a little older it became apparent that he suffered from cryptorchidism and that would keep him out of the show ring for the rest of his life. As a matter of fact, the kennel owners were seriously considering destroying him. If it weren't for George Atkins, the local mailman, Mortimer would never have seen his fifth month.

George wanted a large dog to walk his mail route with him for company and for protection from other dogs that always attacked him. For two years George and Mortimer delivered mail together and had a great time. One day a film crew showed up in the small town to shoot a commercial. The director of the unit decided he wanted a dog in the background after he spotted Mortimer and George Atkins walking their mail route. The owners of the product being advertised in the commercial liked Mortimer's looks and personality and asked for a commercial using the dog as the main character. The rest is show-business history. From TV commercials to a TV series to a string of successful motion pictures was the story of "Mortimer —Everybody's Dog."

George Atkins had the good sense not to accept the $5,000 offered to him by the original director. And so, Mortimer and George lived in Beverly Hills in a house with a swimming pool, protected from the public by iron gates, private guards, and patrol dogs. Of course, George gave up his mail route, but the Postal Service gave him a special status so that he would not lose his pension. After all, you never know. In exchange, George gave the Postal Service the right to use Mortimer's image as "The Postman's Friend," a poster hanging on post-office walls everywhere.

George loved Mortimer as he did in the past, when they simply delivered mail together; but as the dog became an important star, George began relating to the dog from an attitude of inferiority. The relationship really started to deteriorate when George began knocking on the door before entering a room where Mortimer was lying around. Of course, the studio representative's snide attitude toward George was an important inhibiting factor in the relationship. The studio man was intolerant and distant with George and made him feel in the way. The former mailman was constantly excusing himself (even to the dog) as he indulged the animal's every whim. All the dog seemed to want, however, was to see more of George, who was trying to stay out of his way.

Mortimer was now a movie star, and like many people, George was intimidated by this—so intimidated that he lost sight of the fact that Mortimer was a dog and he was a human being. "Pack" status was now all twisted around. George had given up his leadership position, which might have been fine if they were both wolves living in the wild.

Little by little, the representatives of the studio took over the care and maintenance of the dog star. With bruised feelings of inferiority, George retreated to his part of the house and appeared only now and again to sign contracts. He missed the dog terribly and the dog missed him, but he was too depressed to understand what was happening. He no longer supervised Mortimer's diet.

No longer took him for walks. No longer spent those harrowing hours giving the big fellow baths and brushings. George felt it was better that the studio pros do those things. After all, Mortimer was now an important public figure, and what would he want with a common mailman? It was the warm, loving contact of those daily brushings that Mortimer missed most of all. He did not understand why his master rarely touched him anymore.

With George no longer an obstacle, the studio publicity department started scheduling one public appearance after another. The dog's appearances were now booked five and six days at a time. They'd fly him in a private jet across the country to ride in an open-top limousine as the grand marshal of some parade and then fly him to another city for the opening ceremonies of a humane shelter. The dog was pushed and shoved and carted and petted and oohed and aahed with no regular eating schedule and certainly no time for himself.

On the set, it was the same. Just as the script was getting good and Mortimer was supposed to do something interesting, the director would yell "Cut" and call for the stunt dogs. Poor Mortimer was starting to feel as useful as Trigger, stuffed and mounted in Roy Rogers' backyard.

All communication between Mortimer and George ceased, and this had a profound emotional effect on the large dog. When a dog lives with one human for five years and has been subordinate to that person, it is no easy adjustment to accept a reversal of roles and finally a rupture in the relationship. Mortimer missed the loving hands that fed, walked, bathed, brushed, and disciplined him. He was a dog, and he missed his master. He hadn't the slightest idea that humans had transformed him into a film deity. Whenever he saw himself on the screen, he thought he was looking at another dog. When confronted with a crowd of fans, he searched for the one face that he wanted to see the most. He was constantly disappointed and it began to take its toll. The large Saint Bernard was beginning to feel the physical consequences of emotional stress and lack of proper care.

It was about this time that the trouble began. Mortimer was being groomed for a scene that he was to shoot in one hour. To the groomer's horror he found two bald patches about the size of a dime on Mortimer's forehead. At the same time, one of the handlers told the director that the dog had not touched his food all day and that the star was lethargic and disinterested in everything.

A veterinarian was summoned immediately and, to the embarrassment of everyone on the set, a rectal temperature reading was taken. The crew immediately set up some screens to give the dog privacy. The vet told the studio head, who had by this time dropped everything and come down to the set, that Mortimer had demodectic mange, caused by tiny mites that burrow tunnels into the skin and cause the loss of fur, underneath which was red, scaly skin. The vet said that it was not serious for the moment, but that Mortimer would have to have much of his coat shaved off so that other infected parts of the body could be seen and treated. The doctor was indignant and spoke harshly. The dog was run down, and that was probably the main cause of the disease. It was pointed out that Mortimer had put on too much weight, did not seem to be getting a balanced diet and that his muscle tone was atrocious.

"How much exercise does this animal get?" asked the vet. No one answered.

"No one knows," muttered the doctor. "Okay, how many walks in a day does he get?" There was no answer. In truth, no one knew because no one exercised the dog. He was allowed to relieve himself anywhere he wanted to, so he didn't even get walked for that purpose.

"This dog is a physical wreck. Who's responsible for

his welfare?" asked Dr. Bolton looking into the crowd of studio representatives.

"George Atkins, I guess," answered one of the executives.

"Well," said the vet, "you get him over and take this dog home. He's gonna need a new set of ears when I get through with him. I'll tell you, I'll get a court order and have the SPCA come get this animal unless he isn't taken better care of."

"Where the hell is George Atkins?" shouted the studio head. "Send a car for him. You tell us what to do, doc, and it'll be done."

In a cowed and conciliatory manner, the head of the studio pleaded with George Atkins to step back into the picture and take care of his dog once again. At first the old letter carrier was reluctant to get involved.

"Mortimer is an important dog, and I wouldn't want to interfere with his life. There's no dignity being supported by a dog, you know."

The studio head was irritated. He replied. "You damn fool. That dog needs you. Don't you see what's happening to him? For God's sake, he's falling apart!"

George wiped his eyes and blew his nose and gave the matter serious consideration. His reply was given slowly and with much emotion.

"I love that old boy and wouldn't want any harm to come to him. I guess I'll just let him know that. Where is he now?"

Within minutes the old "pack" was reunited and put on the old footing. Both George and Mortimer immediately began to feel better.

With a lot of care and attention, Mortimer's mange began to heal. Twice a week the Saint Bernard was given a mineral oil bath and then dabbed with a liquid medication. Of course he looked awful with half his long coat shaved off. He resembled a barber's pole with a face. The handsome movie star was the worst he had ever looked in his life.

A sensible nutritional regimen was established: a good balance of high-quality protein, fat, carbohydrates, vitamins, and minerals. Catered buffets and exotic people-food were removed from the dog's diet. In addition, George saw to it that the dog was exercised every day. But probably the most important aspect of Mortimer's cure was the reestablishment of his relationship with George Atkins. His owner suffered much guilt about the dog's poor health and worked very hard to make up for lost time. He wasn't about to let Mortimer down again.

George's answer to the problem was to get himself reinstated with the Postal Service. He was given a short mail route in the exclusive community of Beverly Hills. The reason for taking another mail route was for Mortimer's sake. Every morning and every afternoon, plain old George the Mailman hiked up and down the manicured Hills of Beverly followed by his mangy-looking dog, Mortimer. Many a movie star was handed his mail by an equally famous colleague without knowing who it was. No one suspected. Not even the head of Contagion Filmway Studios, who lived down the road. Mortimer's film was held up in production while his fellow actors (and stunt dogs) waited for his long coat to grow back to normal. But somehow it was quite clear that things were going to be different. In the meantime, the mail must go through.

Mortimer was not fed properly, nor did he receive the exercise so important for a dog his size. He was driven to a state of nervous exhaustion by living in an atmosphere of great pressure and tension. Couple that with a lack of affection, and you have the perfect conditions for physical and emotional breakdown. This much stress can cause a great deal more than just demodectic mange. Lack of exercise, poor diet, excess weight, long work hours, disruption of the normal routine, and lack of emotional contact can lead to heart disease, dermatitis, arthritis, allergies, chronic diarrhea, ulcers, viral infections, disorders of the nervous system, and dozens of other ailments and diseases.

———————◆———————

It has been reported that wolves spend one-third of their day traveling, one-third stalking prey, and one-third sleeping. Between summer and winter they may travel as much as 500 miles to keep up with the herd prey. This may explain why wolves, cousins of domestic dogs, are always in lean, hard shape. Only those that go hungry are in as bad shape as many pet dogs. The reason is diet and physical activity.

The wolf travels great distances and works quite hard for his living in the course of one day. This may give us a general idea of the physical activity required by domestic dogs to keep them healthy. There are many factors to consider when determining what the exercise requirements are of individual dogs. Size is certainly an important factor. The larger the body, the more movement it will take to keep the muscles (including the heart) in tone. Weight and daily activity also play a part in one's exercise choices. Weather and climatic conditions are equally important. One of the best ways to determine how much exercise to give a dog is to investigate what employment his breed was developed for. The Saint Bernard, for example, was developed for its strength so that it could successfully work as a rescue dog in the Alps. Its powerful build and acute sense of smell allowed it to rescue thousands of people in past centuries trapped beneath fallen snow in the St. Bernard Pass in Switzerland.

A small lapdog, living indoors in a temperate climate, is certainly not going to require the same amount of exercise as an outdoor sporting dog such as a pointer or an Irish setter. Overweight middle-aged dogs should be exercised more than trim adolescent ones. It's all a matter of common sense.

Although by necessity your dog's exercise is dictated by the time available for it to be given, some aspects of physical activity must be understood. The dog began as an outdoor creature, carving out territory, fighting to keep it, hunting great distances for food, migrating when the food stock migrated, and protecting its young. The domestic version of the wild dog remains possessed by many of the same instincts and resulting physical and emotional needs. All dogs have the instinct to hunt (with or without the talent for it) and build up a great deal of energy that must be released. Like caged animals in the zoo, they must be let out of their apartments and houses and given a workout. It's not only important physically, but emotionally as well.

When considering your dog's exercise, do not be fooled by size. Although most toy breeds require minimal amounts of exercise, some of the small terriers need more than their size would seem to indicate. The smallest of terriers were hunters at one time, and they still have a lot of steam to work off. The working breeds, the hounds, the sporting breeds, many of the terriers (certainly the larger ones), and various nonsporting breeds such as dalmatians, poodles, and schipperkes all need from moderate to vigorous workouts. Remember, working dogs used to labor from eight to fourteen hours a day. Sporting dogs may have run through fields and brush for as far as 20 miles in one morning. All dogs need exercise.

The average dog should be taken outdoors twice a day for a half hour each trip. A two- or three-mile walk/run is about right, plus an opportunity to run loose and jump in a closed-off environment. In large cities, this is difficult at best and impossible at worst. There are compromise measures, however. It is beneficial if you take your dog out whenever an opportunity presents itself. Take him with you on as many chores as possible. This at least satisfies the need to be released from confinement. Play with your dog as often as you can, and make the game very physical—such as throwing a ball or stick for him to retrieve. This can be done indoors. The very best situation is for someone who jogs to allow the dog to participate by tagging along.

Do not exercise an older dog too strenuously. An animal recovering from illness must be allowed to rest and regain strength. Some large to oversized breeds are predisposed to a very serious ailment known as "bloat." It is rare but very serious and can lead to death. Bloat comes after eating and is sometimes connected with strenuous exercise. The stomach may twist in such a way that it prevents expanding gas from leaving the body, and the dog literally swells up like a basketball. It is very painful. If you own a dog as large as a Great Dane or Saint Bernard, it is best to avoid gaseous vegetables such as cauliflower or broccoli. Do not allow your dog to exercise strenuously before or after meals. If symptoms of bloat appear, see a veterinarian immediately.

CHAPTER FIVE

IT'S TRAINING CATS AND DOGS

Dogs

You're walking your dog on a nice, sunny day. A friend greets you and all three of you stop. You say, "Wolfgang, sit." Your dog makes a slight gesture at sitting. He has never been taught the command "sit" and has never been taught the meaning of the word.

A similar system is used by Professor Harold Hill in *The Music Man.* He called it the Think System of teaching music. The only problem with it is that dogs cannot receive mental telepathic messages—at least not in verbal terms.

You start to chew the fat with your friend and become involved in some tidbit of gossip. Wolfgang smells a dried urine spot on the curb, stretches the leash to its fullest, and jerks for the invisible deliciousness. You pull him back in the middle of who's doing it to whom and in a very annoyed tone whine, "Sit." A cute cocker spaniel waddles by flapping her ears and tail in the middle of who died and of what cause. Wolfgang goes crackers and bolts for the tantalizing young thing. You jerk him so hard that all fours leave the ground as you shout, "SIT, DAMN IT, SIT!" Wolfgang leaves you alone as you continue your conversation. The talk ends, you say good-bye, and depart. As you step away, you realize that Wolfgang has dumped on your shoe, and suddenly you understand why the Edwardians wore spats and high-button shoes. As the man once said, "What we have here is a failure to communicate."

Make no mistake about it, dog training involves manipulative techniques for altering your dog's behavior patterns. It all depends on how it's done as to whether it has any negative or personality-change effects on both you and the dog. In human terms we run great risks in a personal relationship when we try to manipulate another human being. In training dogs, there is really no other choice because of the animal's limited abilities to understand what you want and expect and, of course, because dogs do not have a language capacity. Manipulation of dog behavior runs quite a gamut from begging on your knees to dastardly physical abuse. A dog that is thrashed soundly may eventually do what is expected, but at a tremendous cost to his dignity, his rights as one of God's creatures, and his delightful potential as a friend and companion. A dog that is thrashed regularly will eventually become dangerous to himself and to the psychoneurotic coward that beats him. In a last stand at dignity, a battered dog will fight back and get a few slashes and tears in before he is disposed of.

Of course, the most common negative training situation is when the dog is treated like a divinity and asked to suffer the poor humans who come as supplicants, begging for his cooperation. Forget it! A young dog's mind has to be played like a harp to make it work for his master. It requires subtlety, consistency, and a sure-footed knowledge of what you are doing.

◆

Wendel McCoy was a professor of English literature at Chapel Hill University in North Carolina. He was one

of those rare men who could heat rolls by talking to
them. His students adored him because he was able to
communicate to them what he had in mind, and what he
had in mind was usually to their liking. One of his newer
and more original teaching themes was "Writers and Their
Pets." It was different and quite captivating to study the
relationships between T. S. Eliot and his cats as revealed
in his *Old Possum's Book of Practical Cats* or Eugene
O'Neill's *The Last Will and Testament of an Extremely
Distinguished Dog*. Paul Gallico, Ogden Nash, James
Thurber, Dickens, Kipling, Twain, Faulkner, Terhune all
lived out their canine and feline literary creations and
had special feelings about them. Virginia Woolf wrote a
biography of Flush, the much-adored cocker spaniel
owned by Elizabeth Barrett Browning. Mackinlay Kantor's
Lobo and Jack London's masterpiece, *The Call of the
Wild*, were all part of the course which was described by
all McCoy's students as "wonderful." At the end of the
year, they bought him an English springer spaniel puppy
because they felt it best suited his personal glow and
tweedy self. The day they presented the little critter, it
was *Goodbye, Mr. Chips* all the way. McCoy was very
touched by the gesture, which he secretly expected. It also
scared the hell out of him. He didn't really like dogs and
knew very little about them and their ways.

He knew enough to spread out newspapers on the
kitchen floor and confine the little guy there at night. But
for many weeks he did little more than that. Somehow the
dog, now named *Kant*, couldn't. He couldn't stop from
chewing the baseboards. He couldn't exercise enough
self-control to avoid lifting his hind leg and watering the
housekeeper's tulip bulbs. He couldn't do one single
thing that was asked of him.

The first time McCoy took him out, he tied a stylish
red bandanna around the dog's neck instead of a sturdy
leather collar. Then the good professor tied an eight-foot

piece of manila hemp around the bandanna to serve as
one of the longest puppy leashes in recorded history. All
the dog needed was a sombrero and a gold tooth and he
could have been cast in a remake of *The Treasure of the
Sierra Madre*. It was particularly busy on the town streets,
with a great deal of car and truck traffic. McCoy carried
the puppy to the sidewalk and set him down with great
expectations of taking a casual constitutional . . . just **a**
man and his dog.

As the dog touched the sidewalk, a rattling pickup
truck in dire need of a new muffler quaked its way up the
street. The little dog ran the full eight feet of the yellow
rope and cringed in terror against the nearest wall. McCoy
was almost dragged off his feet. He pulled at the rope,
gently at first, trying to get the dog to walk. Kant shivered
as he tried to integrate into the wall. With determined
force McCoy yanked the leash, but still the dog wouldn't
budge. Finally, with all his might, he jerked the rope and
socked his own jaw with both his fists, which were tightly
clutched. For an instant the scholarly dog owner saw
stars and heard bells. Having recovered, he carried the
dog home noticing that his paws had been scraped against
the sidewalk so hard that there was a little blood showing
through the pads.

The next step in the little dog's education was to
teach his master that he didn't want to come to him every
time he was called. "C'mon, Kant, let's go, boy. Here.
Come here, will you please? Mr. McCoy's got a biscuit
for you." Success. All McCoy had to do was pull out a dog
biscuit and the dog would appear at his feet with all the
loyalty of a nineteenth-century camel driver. The small
springer had a real craving for the cookielike biscuits
and was a sucker for a bribe. However, if the good professor was not prepared with payola when he called
the dog, nothing happened. The young extortionist would
barely turn away from his current activity, which could be

anything from eating the couch to claiming a far wall
with his hind leg raised. The unflappable Wendel McCoy
would quietly walk away from the indifferent dog like an
experimenter going back to the drawing board. The principal difference was that he never had a new or better idea
how to communicate with the animal. It never occurred
to him that he should be the dominant figure in their relationship. He conducted his pet stewardship in strictly
egalitarian terms. He thought it was the democratic thing
to do. What actually existed was a dog dictatorship with
he, the human, brought to his knees with a paw on his
neck. It was not so much a humiliation as it was a boring
waste of time.

Finally, McCoy's three-times-a-week housekeeper,
Mrs. Gladys Coldstream, had a showdown.

"Dr. McCoy," she started out as she braced herself
against the edge of the sink, "something's got to change
here."

"What are you talking about?"

"That little beast with the liver-flap ears, that's what
I'm talking about. So far he's eaten my electric orange
juicer, half of my mixer, an entire spatula, and the hose
off your Water-Pick. And that's not to mention the crap-
pola neatly positioned at the base of my tulip stems. You
don't have a sock left without a hole in the toe, and he's
twice stepped into biscuit batter." The old gray workhorse
with her solid square jaw began to cry.

"If you don't do something about that rotten dog,
(she shouts) I WILL!"

"What can you do? What would you do?"

"Oh," she said, shaking her head and her fist, "I'd give
him a dog lesson. Don't you see, he's got to be made to
understand about dogs and people."

"How'd you like to explain that to me?" said McCoy.

"It's really very simple. The first time he gets out of

line, you step on his neck and holler like hell. Eventually
he'll get the idea."

McCoy rubbed his chin, hoping an answer would come
out of his mouth like a penny fortune. He didn't like the
sound of what Coldstream had in mind.

"I think you'd better let me handle it."

"Sure," she yelled, "you handle it—or I will. Remember, my foot three feet up you-know-what."

Later that evening, after a cold dinner, McCoy decided
that if he could tame cages full of undergraduates, there
was no reason why he couldn't get through to a simple-
minded *Canis familiaris*. "Say what you have in mind in
the most honest and sincere fashion, with firmness and
reason," he thought. "Sure, have a talk with the poor fellow. No wonder he doesn't do anything right. We don't
understand each other. Most assuredly he'll apply himself
to the problem at hand once I explain that he's not working up to his full potential. Yes, that's it. We'll have a talk.
And when it's over, he'll understand that my success is
determined by how well he does around here. It's on him."

Feeling an expansive glow, McCoy left his coffee cup
on the arm of his stuffed chair and went looking for
Kant.

"Hey, boy. Yo, Kant. Where are you, kiddo?"

Kant did not answer.

With glasses in hand, he searched throughout the
small cottage but could not find one trace of the adolescent
springer. Deciding to warm up to the heart-to-heart before they sat down, McCoy yelled out, "Oh, Kant. Did
you know that the word *spaniel* literally means a Spanish
dog. And *springer* derives from Old English *spring*, itself
from Old English *springan*, to leap, whence, via Middle
English *springen*, and finally to the English 'to spring,'
occasionally used as *sprung*. That must mean you are an
Hispanic canine with a predisposition toward jumping on

things. Logic, my friend. That's what makes the world turn 'round. Logic."

With that the horn-rimmed logician entered the inner sanctum of his bedroom. There he found Kant sitting next to his chest of drawers. It dated back to 1609. The elaborate chest was hand carved, painted and ornamented with Elizabethan strapwork inlaid into the brightly painted wood. It was an especially rare and expensive piece of furniture.

McCoy began rubbing his hand when he saw the results of Kant's preoccupation. Half the patina was licked away from the third drawer from the top. The lower two drawers had the painted wood surfaces chewed off the base material to reveal that it was only a veneer covering hardwood underneath. The mutilated chest was a fake and not worth fussing over what the dog had done to it. McCoy felt as though a bell clapper struck him first on one side of his head and then the other. He did not pass out as he should have. He tore at the bulging vein in his neck and shrieked out something that sounded like "Spanish swine." With two arms extended like a frothing madman wanting to strangle, he chased the dog around the house. There was smashing and kicking and yelling and puppy howling and finally low-throated sobbing. Their talk was over. The next day Wendel McCoy went on a two-year sabbatical and Kant went to live with Mrs. Coldstream. She was determined to teach him about dogs and people and tulip stems.

Training a dog can be an emotional business if you are not working from sound principles and techniques. There are three training facts that the good professor McCoy did not understand about dog training. One: a dog is genetically organized to live and function within the demands of a pack structure based on dominance and subordination. Two: the ideal time to create within the animal a susceptibility to obedience training is precise and predetermined. And three: there is a teaching process which is based on the Pavlovian principles of conditioned reflexes reinforced with rewards and punishments (replace the word punishments with corrections).

Dogs do not have the mental capacities of human beings, obviously, and therefore nothing Wendel McCoy could have said to his dog would have made the slightest difference in dog training. To merely tell a dog to sit on command means nothing. He must be *taught* how to sit and made to associate the utterance of the word with the action of sitting. The action must then be reinforced with a pleasant reward, thus conditioning him to do as you command out of an uncontrollable desire to obey. If it sounds like mind bending, that's exactly what it is. It is also referred to as behavior modification.

One need only study the social structure of the wolf pack to understand the most basic life-style of the domestic dog. Sometimes wolf packs are comprised of blood relations and sometimes combinations of relatives and close neighbors of circumstance. Hunting, mating, and carving out territory, the essentials for survival in the wild, are accomplished as a group effort. However, there is a chain of command involving a leader of the pack and the various lesser lights of the pecking order. The leader is determined by size and the pugnaciously won right to lead. Once the lead wolf is determined, the lower-ranking wolves sort themselves out and find themselves relegated to various tasks and privileges based on rank.

This life-style is basic from the first waking moments of a domestic dog's life. Entering into a human/canine situation does not alter the dog's instincts. He merely transfers the instinct for social structure to the human condition and transposes the idea of "pack" into the more familiar condition known as "family." Now, his instinct is to either lead the family (pack) or be led by the strongest member(s). From the dog's point of view, a leader is absolutely necessary, and he will take the job if only by default of the human members of the pack. The dog's instinct for survival forces him to fill the position of leader if no member of the family takes the responsibility. Therefore, in order to train a dog, he must be relegated to the status of subordinate family member rather than dominant member—or he will not even attempt to learn or obey.

It is now widely accepted that there are critical phases in the earliest weeks of a puppy's life that help shape his ability to be influenced by various environmental factors. The first three weeks (21 days) of a puppy's life are spent developing his sensory and motor capacities. Between the fourth and thirteenth weeks, the adaptability to social relationships is determined if certain conditions are or are not present in the puppy's immediate sensory environment. Isolation during this period will not permit the animal to develop an adaptability to humans or other dogs.

A dog kept exclusively with other dogs and never introduced to humans during this stage will adapt only to the presence of other dogs *throughout his life!* If the dog is exposed to human contact, both sensory and emotional, during this critical period (4–13 weeks), he will become extremely adaptable to human family life and consequently susceptible to obedience training. This is called "socializing." Based on the research of Dr. John Fuller and Dr. Jean Paul Scott, the optimum time to remove a puppy from its litter is at the end of the seventh week of life. Between eight and sixteen weeks the dog is not only entering its prime time for adapting to the idea of human acceptance, it is also ready to have circumstances develop the dominant or subordinate inclination with its pack or family. It is then that obedience training has its best opportunity for effectiveness without disturbing the little dog's emotional stability.

Teaching a dog obedience training is a lengthy and technical process, one which cannot be covered in these limited pages. The underlying principles can be given, however, so that almost any manual can be obtained and utilized with utmost efficiency.

When training a dog, the dominant/subordinate relationship is of primary concern. The human being clearly must take a leadership position, and this is accomplished by understanding that you, the human, are the responsible adult in the situation and that your pet is a totally dependent dog. Your voice must be firm and resonant when giving obedience commands (especially during the training sessions). You must maintain a no-nonsense attitude like a commanding officer dealing with a private in the army. Your dog's willingness to obey your commands may save his life some day in a potentially hazardous traffic situation. An obedience-trained dog is less likely to lose his good home or run away and get himself stolen or ensnared by a dog warden.

Taking the dominant position with a puppy is the easiest thing in the world. Simply make him follow you everywhere. Call him to you in a friendly tone of voice (not too exuberantly). Few puppies can resist this. When he runs up to your legs, turn around and begin walking away. He should follow. Walk a few steps and bend down and pet him and reward him with praise. Repeat this command many times throughout the day. You will be conditioning the animal to follow you and thus take a secondary position with you. His reward is your praise and approval. In this way you have automatically taken the position of pack leader and circumvented the dog's need or desire to take it himself. Once you have assumed that role, you must always play it.

(Assuming that you have taken the pack-leader position with your young dog, and given that he is "socialized" at the eighth week of life, you are ready to create a perfectly obedience-trained animal.) Using the command "sit" as an example lesson, you must physically force the dog (in a firm but gentle manner) into the sitting position as you say the word.

Push the dog's posterior with your left hand while holding the dog's head by raising the leash slightly upward. Say "sit" in a firm, commanding voice as you do this. Each time the dog is physically forced into the sitting position, praise him lavishly and tell him how good he is. Repeat this command ten, fifteen, or even twenty times during a ten-minute training session. Once your dog seems to understand what the word "sit" means, he may be commanded without being physically positioned. If he obeys the word without being pushed into it, praise him immediately. If he does not obey your vocal command, correct him with a slight jerk of the leash and say "no" firmly. Your dog should sit after the word "No." If he does, praise him. If he doesn't, begin the teaching process over again.

This is precisely how a conditioned reflex is created. An adaptable puppy or adolescent dog seeks your approval and can be taught obedience training by your giving or withholding of praise and by the implementation of correction or punishment gestures, almost always involving a slight side jerk of the leash. Repetition, consistent pack-leader status, rewards, and corrections comprise the formula for simple obedience training. Although it is unthinkable to condition a human being in such oversimplified, manipulative terms, it is a blessing for the dog living in a human family. Here your dog experiences absolute clarity about what is expected of him so that he may live a happy, untroubled existence. Dogs and humans prefer it that way.

Cats

If there are such lunatics known as cat-haters as opposed to cat-lovers then surely the issues of obedience training entwine around such madness.

"What did he say?"

"He said that a lot of people don't like cats because they're too damned independent."

Can it be a coincidence that Napoleon, the great military genius who ate half the world, was terrified of cats? He was the classic ailurophobe who broke out into cold sweats at the mere sight or suggestion of a cat. Perhaps their independence and attitude toward discipline gave him nightmares of French armies rejecting basic training and front-line duty? And during the Dark Ages, didn't Europe persecute cats as agents of the devil who would take no special notice of humankind's wants or desires?

It is a speculation to ponder that entrenched ailurophobes develop their irrational emotions simply because cats will not, can not, should not bend their collective will to the collective enforcement of petty human tyrants, bullies, and megalomaniacs. However, every cat has his price and will accept some training and discipline under the right circumstances. Give a little, get a little.

———◆———

Harlan Keebler, known to his many baseball fans as the Cookie Monster, was married for six years. The right fielder from Philadelphia, in his early thirties, was starting to look at other women, especially when the team went out on the road during the season. Although neither he nor his wife Lorraine mentioned the danger to their relationship, they were both aware of the problem. He was lonely, he was famous, there was a lot of tension to shake after a tough game and . . . the out-of-town temptation was there. So she got him a cat!

"What's this?" he asked with a grin, looking at the toffee-colored sylph with its chocolate-colored points.

Lorraine grinned intelligently and answered, "Your new roomie for the season. I thought you could stand some company since they won't let me soothe the savage breast for you."

"Okay, but I warn you she's going to be some real competition."

"I'll take my chances," Lorraine bubbled into her coffee cup. "You got time for a second cup or something?" Harlan smiled as he toyed with his pajama button. He nodded.

"What'll we call it?"

Her eyes popped, "What?"

"The cat. It needs a name."

"Oh, she has a name. Someone thought that Homeplate was appropriate."

He laughed. "Very clever."

The season began with six out-of-town games lost for the Philadelphia team. Cookie Keebler was hitting .281 for the series but cost the team three errors in the field. His last one was an easy pop fly that just missed his glove and allowed two runs on a double. The game went into an extra inning, but he struck out and ended the game. Nobody said a kind word in the locker room. He went to his hotel, took a shower, had a small dinner, and curled up in front of the TV with Homeplate in his lap. He was miserable, but the cat was more so. She didn't like staying in a strange hotel room by herself and was not afraid to let her attitude on the subject be known.

The phone rang. It was Lorraine calling from Philadelphia. She wanted to console him but only managed to irritate him further by discussing the things that went wrong on the field. She was trying to cover up his not calling her in two days. It had her guessing. After he told her flatly that he didn't want to discuss the game anymore, there was a long silence between them. She broke it.

"How's the cat?"

"Rotten. It was a rotten idea. They're not so independent after all."

"What do you mean? All cats are independent. Just give them a dish of food and forget it."

"Bull. She was so grateful to see the chambermaid after I left for the game this afternoon, she damn near knocked her down. If the woman wasn't a fan of mine, she'd have sued. The cat doesn't like being left alone."

"Well," said Lorraine, "then don't leave her alone."

"Hey, we're talking about game time now."

"Well, get her a sitter." End of conversation.

With his face burning red, Harlan shaved, broke out his new pearl-gray suit, petted the cat goodnight and made a beeline for the hotel lounge. The tall athlete was honey for the bar flies. He pulled up a stool and three men in blue herringbone suits (wearing garters for sure) gathered around him interfering with his sightline of a barmaid with a silky black uniform and lavender lace handkerchief on her lapel. It was the handkerchief that got him. He almost broke his neck trying to see around the three herringbones slapping his back, refilling his glass, and telling him about the year Philadelphia won the pennant.

She must have waited two hours before approaching the half-potted ballplayer, twinkling her eyes and saying, "Is there anything I can do for you, Mr. Keebler?"

At last his trading stamps were to be redeemed for the big prize. Fame and fortune were about to show three cherries and release a jackpot. He leaned just a bit to the side of the stool, but didn't know it. His left hand held tightly to the edge of the mahogany bar—and a good thing, too.

"Yeah," he said. "You busy later?"

"I'm off in fifteen minutes."

"So?"

"So I'm not busy."

"Oh, yeah. Look," he smiled with a sweating forehead, "I'm right here in the hotel. Room 782. If you can make it, why don't you just slip right up the old elevator and have something or other with me?"

"I'd love it."

Cookie paid his check, slipped out of the lounge, and made his way home via the elevator. He tore his room key out of his pants pocket with sweating hands and fussed at the door until he got it to unlock. He sailed into the dark room stripping off his tie and coat in a mad dash across the floor. He stumbled over something on the floor. Feeling along the wall he found the light switch. Once the lamp was lit, he looked around and saw pure wreckage.

The large stuffed chair was turned over on its side. Picture frames were askew; one even had the glass frame cracked. The lamp on his night table was on its back— broken, of course. The long stretch of draperies covering the picture window was shredded near the bottom, as were various parts of the bright blue carpet. The caddy with the large suitcase still in it was down, with under- wear, shirts, and athletic supporters scattered everywhere. Just then a knock on the door stopped the buzzing in Cookie's head. The doorknob turned, and in walked the lavender handkerchief. Her cheeks and lips were new and smiling. She stepped into the center of the mess and took a silent look at everything. Standing to the side was Keebler holding a note of explanation that was placed on his bed. She shook her head and slipped out, taking her perfume and handkerchief with her.

"Oh, no," she muttered. "This ain't for me."

Keebler hardly noticed her exit as he read the note:

Dear Mr. Keebler.

About your cat. It seems that she cannot bear to be without you. After several hours and no less than fifteen

*complaints concerning the horrible sounds coming from
your room, we had no choice but to enter your room to
learn what indescribable crime was being committed
against the person of some defenseless creature. Having
discovered that it was a lonely and desperate cat of the
Siamese persuasion, we attempted to lock her in the
bathroom. A struggle ensued, the results which you
are no doubt standing in the middle of. Please, Mr.
Keebler, after you've paid your bill in the morning,
would you mind removing yourself from this hotel—
or flushing your brown friend down the toilet. Frankly,
both gestures would be appreciated.*

> *Hospitably yours,*
>
> *Bill Buchhausen,*
> *Manager*

Standing atop a pile of athletic supporters, the cat
would not look him in the eye. Instead she decided to
lick her paws and haunches clean. With each long slurp
she would look up at the big man and adore him with a
slight squeeze of her eyes. He watched her in silence for a
full minute and then said, "You know what, Homeplate?
You need some bush-league training on how to be a cat
in the majors." In a slow and deliberate movement, he un-
tied his polished black shoe and slipped it off his foot. In
one frenzied dive, he swung at Homeplate with the shoe
in an effort to slam her good and hard.

Easily avoiding the shoe, the cat leaped instantly
to a false marble mantelpiece. With frustrated rage he
barely escaped falling on his face. "Commere, you miserable beast. Don't you want any cat training?" He swung
again, but Homeplate jumped again and crawled under
the bed and became two tiny flecks of yellow staring out
at the madman. As he swung at the cat, he banged his
elbow against the hard surface and felt his shoulder
muscle pull with pain. "Yeeagh! I'm injured! Oh, no.

I've injured myself." He sat down on the bed and tried to move his arm around. Eventually it moved in all directions as it was supposed to. He shook his head with relief and groaned, "Homeplate, what do you want from me? Give me a break, will you?"

He called his wife and informed her that he was dropping the animal into some wet concrete at a construction site. "The best thing you can do with this animal is let her become the cornerstone of some building."

Lorraine replied hysterically, "If you harm one hair of that cat, I won't be here when you get back."

Keebler thought about it and said, "I'm dropping her off at a shelter or something, then."

"Look," said Lorraine, "I'll find out what you can do about her, but in the meantime don't do anything. She's a good cat and you just have to give her time to adjust to your crazy life-style. God knows, I still haven't been able to. Just don't leave her alone until you get back in town, and I'll take care of the rest."

With that, she hung up the phone quickly before he could say another word. "Hey!" Too late. He was stuck.

The team moved from city to city, working its way across the country, but Harlan Keebler did not once leave his hotel room. He couldn't afford the repair bills. Neither he nor Homeplate strayed even once. The sweet kitty-cat never made a fuss as long as Cookie was there to hold and pet the oriental darling. When he left to play ball, he packed the lump of brown candy into her carrier and let her watch the game from the dugout. She even accompanied him to restaurants, where she was given her own chair at the table, provided that she remained in her bubble-top case. The big ballplayer once took her to a bar, but for some reason the smell of the booze didn't agree, and triggered off a loud stream of embarrassing merrrowwws. He packed the cat up in a hurry and beat it out of the place.

After three weeks on the road, the Philadelphia team finally made it home, where dozens of wives and girlfriends waited at the airport. Harlan, Lorraine, and Homeplate entered the Federal style town house in midtown and made themselves comfortable as they caught up with lost time.

"So, how'd you make out with Homeplate?"

"She's quite a cat. She tore up every hotel room I had to leave her in. It cost us a fortune in damages."

"Really? We'll fix that. She just needs training. You know, obedience lessons and disciplining. She'll be good, I know she will. I never heard of a cat that couldn't be left alone."

"Can you train a cat?"

"I bought some books on the subject. They claim it can be done if you work at it."

"I'd like that," said Harlan with a less than sincere tone.

"I'll start the lessons myself. If she's such good company for you, it will be well worth it," said Lorraine, hugging the chocolatey baggage. "Then you can leave the hotel room anytime you want to."

"I can? That's great," said the Cookie Monster with a funny smile on his face as he played with a lilac petal that fell to the lace doily under the bowl. Homeplate let out one of her awful merrrowwws.

In the case of Cookie Keebler and his cat Homeplate, **the** devastation and unruliness were the result of the cat's boredom and complete lack of imposed restraint. A well-fed, trained cat with several toys, including a scratch post, would not have caused quite so much trouble. It is a fact of life that Siamese cats are noisy, talkative creatures when they become lonely or bored and are quite capable of tearing across a room, ravaging as they go. The problem is that they crave attention almost like dogs and suffer from lack of affection and human communication. Some simple training might have solved the problem. A brief understanding of your cat's wild side helps.

Although the domestic cat physically resembles the smaller wild cat it is very much derivative of all the wild felids and their unique behavior traits. Of all the wild cats, two species are very different from the rest. Lions and cheetahs are radically different in various physical ways and in some skills and behavior. The most striking difference between lions and other cats is that they live and hunt in groups or prides, much as wolves do. A pride of lions often consists of many females and their cubs, a few males, and one dominant lion, the king of the jungle (or at least of the pride). The male lion is the only cat in nature that wears the rich golden-brown mane which adds that royal look so much admired and found on royal and aristocratic seals. All other cats, wild and domestic, are solitary figures, hunting and living alone and coming together only for the purpose of mating and other parental chores. Perhaps our domestic cat's ability to live in a human setting is somehow related to the lion's tendency to live in a social structure. It would explain the house cat's duality of dependency and independency, but only up to a point.

Cheetahs do not have the large, sharp, retractible claws for primary weapons that all other cats do. They cannot climb trees with the grace and ease of other cats—including the humble tabby—unless it is out of desperation. They do not even have the powerful jaws or great teeth that other felids have, and their muzzles are like those of dogs. As a result, cheetahs must learn as cubs to take careful aim and bite or strangle the throat of a prey animal if they want to eat. They are slender, awkward animals with long, slim legs. However, when they spring into action, there are no animals in nature to match them. Cheetahs are the fastest animals alive. They spring to speeds of 45 miles per hour in less than two seconds and can clock speeds of 70 miles per hour for short distances. It is in the chase that their dull claws become an asset, lending traction like cleated shoes. Although cheetahs sometimes hunt in family groups (mostly mothers and cubs), they are solitary animals. They do not live in the social structure of a pride. Perhaps your own cat's tear across the living room is reminiscent of the cheetah?

There are many minor differences between all wild cats, such as the tiger's proclivity for swimming and nomadic, nonterritorial existence; or the leopard's wily tricks for fooling potential game and its extraordinary tree-climbing ability, where much of its eating is accomplished. But much of the wild feline behavior is similar and has great bearing on the training behavior of the common house cat.

Most house cats, like most wild cats, are not pack- or herd- or pride-oriented creatures. That doesn't mean that they aren't gregarious and friendly from time to time. The so-called independent allure of the cat is based on its genetically organized behavior toward hunting and other matters pertaining to survival. All cats hunt for a living, including the most can-opener-oriented beggars. It is a fever in the blood pertaining to survival and must be allowed if and when the opportunity arises. Stalking, hunting, and eating are of primary concern to all cats, and it is this obsession that gives the civilized cat owner the only shot at something mildly resembling obedience-training opportunities.

Your cat needs you as a primary source of food and accepts that reality with a grudging dependence. It's a question of shriveling ecology. Once the feeding patterns are established, short customs soon become hardened habits that are difficult to change. Given the first coded message of behavior that food is on its way, your cat, unless ill, becomes excited and impatient. It is between the first gesture and the actual serving of the food that all good cat training is effective. With many social types, the offer of affection has the same effect.

It is important to understand the great limitations of cat training. Whereas a dog will learn to heel, sit, come, lie down, roll over, stay, and many other commands, cats barely do what you want—and on a limited basis only. They do not crave your approval, nor get delirious over being told "That's a good boy!" They are exceedingly intelligent beings with a marvelous problem-solving ability in some respects superior to that of dogs. They will allow themselves to be taught a few commands only if there is some advantage pertaining to food or other *tangible* reward.

The most important training for cats consists of teaching them to know their own names; to come when called; to accept housebreaking (litter-pan use); to learn the command "No!" All the rest are merely parlor tricks that have no purpose other than entertainment.

When training a cat, you must become aware of the tone of your voice. A soft, friendly sound is best. Never soft-soap a cat into coming to you so that you can then punish him in any way, or he will not come to you the next time. When you *sound* friendly, be certain that you *are* friendly. During the training sessions, never call a cat to you without offering a bribe of food or some much-appreciated reward.

Your cat is a unique and individualistic creature and has been an inspiration to writers and painters and sculptors for centuries. Therefore it should not be too difficult to select a name that expresses something of the cat that you like, that you can say with warmth and pride, like Teddy, Euclid, Sal, Custard, Leontine, Divine, Big Mac, or MacMuffin.

If you have been lucky, your pet has been "socialized" as a young kitten and thus made adaptable to the human condition and the mild requests made by cat owners. This simply means that in the early weeks of its life, the cat was held and cuddled several times a day by a human being and then removed from its litter at around eight to ten weeks of age so that it gained a healthy attitude toward people and other cats as well.

Teach your cat its name simply by calling the animal by name at opportune times during the day and evening. A call to dinner is the most effective time to teach its name. Each time the name is used, a food reward must be offered. Once your cat learns its name, it is almost trained for Come When Called. However, for this command, the bribery should be for high stakes in order to properly reinforce the idea. When declaring, "Come on, Cocoa," a reward of some truly adored treat should be offered, such as a yeast pill (they love yeast pills), catnip, cheese omelet, or wheat grass.

The command "No!" is a negatively learned lesson, but perhaps the most valuable one in the repertoire. Walking on your supper, climbing the curtains, using your leg or your couch for a scratch post demands a firmly taught respect for the command "No!" Whenever your cat transgresses, lift him by the scruff of the neck as his mother would do, support his back legs with your palm, shake his head, and use the word "No" in a firm voice.

When a cat behaves in a manner that is disturbing to humans, such as going off house training, or tearing through the living room like a lunatic, or destroying property, something is definitely happening, but not necessarily what we think. Your cat's odd or destructive behavior means something—but not in human terms. It probably has more to do with genetically organized behavior or some deficiency in the environment. For example, if a cat has a great need to roam and that need is thwarted, it may do some damage in the house. The damage may be done not to spite you, but perhaps as a result of trying to get out. It may be scratching the curtains or woodwork in some irrational attempt to get through the wall. When a dog or a cat has an overpowering need to get out of the house (perhaps to respond to a female in heat), it may inflict great damage to the home in that effort. But this must not be misinterpreted as having a destructive or spiteful nature. A cat may suddenly develop an urgent need and respond to it in the only way it can. This is part of the animal's nature and must be understood and accepted as such by the pet owner.

Destructive behavior can often be solved simply by redirecting the cat's actions to some more desirable place. For example, when the puss decides to sharpen its claws on your best armchair, take him to his own scratch post (a nice tall one with a large base), squeeze his paws to expose the claws, and then force them to scratch the proper material. You can never stop a cat from scratching; it is connected with various health and behavior activities. You simply redirect the action. The cat must learn to use the post daily and stay away from valuable furniture, and that requires constant supervision and redirection until the problem no longer exists. This same training principle applies to all negative behavior. Eventually, the cat will learn to stop whatever wrongdoing it is engaged in at the sound of your firm "No!" Do not forget your clubhouse bribe after each encounter. When the cat stops doing something negative, thank him and give him a reward—perhaps a cooked lima bean or a baked Alaska—whatever gets you through the night.

CHAPTER SIX

SEX (Any Pet Can!)

Dogs

Your dog consists of bones, muscles, organs, skin, hair, blood, miscellaneous moisture, an electrical system, and an elaborate chemical composition. Dog behavior is tremendously influenced by this physical life as well as by a genetically organized set of instincts coupled with environmental influences. This miraculous feat of divine engineering involves thousands, maybe millions of various intricate functions of the body, not the least of which is cell reproduction and the body's ability to save its own life from the invasions of sickness. Why then all the fuss about getting your dog fixed up with a sultry Ms. or a big daddy stud? Sex is but one lonely function of the mammalian body. It is true that reproduction seems to be the primary force in all of nature. The reasons for this take us by the hand down pathways of philosophy, religion, and the greater questions of existence. But unless you are involved with procreation in order to further some great idea, your dog's genitalia need never come out of the box, so to speak. This, of course, poses the perennial question of many pet owners:

"Does my dog need to experience sex for his mental and physical well-being?" I'm not going to tell you—not yet, anyway.

———◆———

On certain nights in July, when the air is warm and the water of the East River is cool a damp, muggy mist tends to fog the evening streets around Sutton Place. The city lamps glow a bright yellow, and the quiet of the lateness seems to amplify every single footstep and occasional tug that slips through the river night. It is a time for lit cigarettes and the clinking against the sidewalk of the metal clips of dog leashes. Shiny leather shoes and dog paws slowly trot through the night on casual missions of search and release. Here and there an occasional meeting takes place in the shadows, and one can only imagine large sums of money being agreed upon and secret meetings being arranged in muffled conversations. Walking a dog on such nights in such streets is a remote but sensual experience. Simon Brace knew all about this, which is why he made the trip every now and again.

He was a serious dresser who wanted to look right even if he was just walking the dog at night. His denim bell-bottoms cut the air with a sharp crease in them, and his tawny boxer was slick and groomed to a spit shine. Toro's great black jowls glistened with health, and his white diamond-shaped chest could be seen from half a block away. The dog was held by a two-foot-long thickness of heavily stitched cowhide that could have made a pair of cowboy boots. They were an elegant but rugged team, Simon and Toro. As they took their light constitutional, they both searched for that special something hidden in half-conscious dreams. Simon's search was made with 20-20 mobility while Toro kept his nose to the ground hoping to find his dream rubbed into the cement in thin layers of bouquet.

It was just another empty walk that night until Toro's head left the curbstones for the first time. With pricked ears he gazed through the mist and looked for whatever was attached to the sound of the other metal clip heading for him and his master. The dog's sudden reaction alerted Simon, who also looked ahead as he slowed his pace. Like two aircraft coming out of the clouds, an elegant cocker spaniel with ears awash and legs in full strut almost collided with brute boxer. The two dogs suddenly hopped around each other like friends in a distant land and encircled their tethers, one in leather the other in silver chain. Simon grabbed a quick glance at the beautiful dog's owner and lost his breath. She was in black crepe and lace with a small diamond hanging from her satin blouse. It was hard to see, but the late-show dog walker didn't need a floodlight to know he was in the presence of a once-a-year find. She was lovely—no, she was grand. Looks, style, a gorgeous dog, and obviously a resident of a good neighborhood. She had everything he dreamed of.

"They're a brilliant sight together, aren't they?" offered the owner of Toro.

Lisa Lorna smiled. "Yes, they are. Cushion is two years old next week. How old is . . ."

"Toro," he said with a deep, cleared throat. "Toro's three. Three and a half exactly—and six days."

She smiled again and he almost fainted. They just stood there under a street light, allowing the uninhibited investigations of the two dogs to fill the void as they each searched for something to say. Finally:

"They seem to like each other."

"They certainly do," answered Lisa, "Cushy is never this friendly. It must be love."

Without doing a cartwheel, Simon answered, "Yeah,"

then laughed with neither grace nor wit.

"Has Toro ever serviced a bitch before?"

Sweat dripped from Simon's palms as he replied hoarsely, "Uh, lots of times. What do you think? Of course he has."

"Good," she answered. "Maybe you'd be interested in allowing me to use him for a stud . . . for Cushion. I think they might make interesting puppies. What's his breed?"

"Boxer."

"Well Cushy is a cocker spaniel. If they had puppies that would make them cock-a-boxers, wouldn't it?"

"I guess."

"So, how do you feel about mating these lovers? I'll give you the pick of the litter."

"I consider it a rare opportunity for Toro and me. This is going to be a good thing for him. A dog in the city shouldn't be allowed to remain celibate for too long. It's bad for the environment. It's a matter of ecology and mental health, you know?"

She nodded affirmatively and said, "Great. Where should we do it?"

He swaggered. "Your place or mine? Ha-ha. A little dog humor."

She rolled her eyes at the humor of the question and replied, "Well, I think it's customary to bring the bitch to the stud's run . . ."

Simon opened his mouth as wide as he ever had in thumping anticipation but could not get his answer out in time. "However," she added, "I've got five rooms, and we'll be able to leave them alone. Unless of course you've got five rooms also?"

Once again the injustice of economics defeated Simon Brace, manager of 53rd Street's Hoof and Antler Male Shop. "No, I don't have five rooms. Listen, let's make it at your place. I mean, what's the difference? It's Cushion and Toro's gig, right?"

Four weeks passed, and the delicate Cushion went into heat on schedule. Calls were made and signals sent like emissaries between the Capulets and the Montagues. Finally, the night of the canine connection fell due. Simon had Toro at the groomer on Second Avenue all afternoon, and he looked it. His coat glistened without a short hair out of place, and the thick, white coat conditioner did its job with alacrity and perfumed efficiency. The great stud was ready for Westminster, if necessary. He stood in near-perfect conformation with all four legs spread apart, all male, all ready. And then he vomited on his anxious owner's black patent boots. He did that sometimes. Nobody ever knew why, but the vet once attributed it to nerves. Simon's trousers, his socks, his leg . . . a mess. He bit his tongue and inner lip several times as he viciously chewed gum and changed clothes. At last, the two swains were at the elevator checking themselves out in the hallway mirror as they waited for 18 to flash to 5 and let them in and cart them away.

They hit the street and walked to First Avenue in an effort to hail a taxi. She was six blocks away and Simon didn't want to give the city an opportunity to spoil a promising evening. Under his arm he had a wooden sampler box of champagne splits resting in a blanket of red satin. It was an evening of new beginnings and certain discoveries, and it just seemed like the right gesture. Many cabs with their empty lights on the roof slowed down as if to pick him up but raced by quickly once having seen the barrel-chested bull of a dog on his thick leather lead. The two studs simply kept walking toward Lisa Lorna's building, having given up the luxury of riding. With the exception of a small dog splat on his black shoe, they arrived safe and near spotless.

The doorman was expecting Brace and Dog and ushered them to the elevator. The doors slid open at the thirtieth floor and they found themselves being let into Lisa's place. She had been standing at her open door waiting to let them in. She seemed as eager as Simon and made the biggest fuss over Toro than he had ever gotten before. The dog just stood in place as if being examined for a hernia with his tongue hanging out and slurping now and again as he breathed heavily from the long walk. Simon handed Lisa the wooden box and instructed her to place it in the fridge. She opened it and cooed, "Let's have a toast . . . to them . . . the lovers!"

"Great."

The room was all peach and satin in a Louis-the-Someone period, and the puffy pillows hissed downward three feet as Simon sat and immediately sank deep into the frame of the couch. Lisa returned with two stemmed glasses shimmering with the golden wine and offered one to the low-riding Simon. She sat on an armchair and for some reason did not sink. He felt as if he was being interviewed for a job. Toro plopped himself at Simon's feet and casually glanced around the room.

Simon winced. "Are you sure Cushion is ready?"

"I'm sure."

"Toro doesn't seem to be responding to the . . . ah . . . aroma of heat. He should be very interested by now, and he doesn't seem to be."

She sipped her champagne and said quickly, "Oh, don't worry about that. I had to spray her with a special atomizer so that the management of the building wouldn't evict me. Believe me, when the time is right, he'll know it." She winked and sipped from her glass again.

The young man drank from his glass, too, but took more in with his eyes than he did with his mouth. He couldn't look away from Lisa, who was especially appealing that night. Under the circumstances, however, she could have been working under the hood of a Mack truck and been appealing to him. The room was hot and his neck was wet with sweat as the gold coin suspended from his large gold chain irritated the few black hairs showing through his exaggerated V-neck shirt. His bright blue pants were tight, and he kept checking for embarrassing, involuntary responses. Lisa was ruffled at the neck in a pale yellow summer dress with tiny white cotton dots that were all that blocked Simon's vision. She took his very breath away. He was sitting at a fixed race, and he held the winning ticket.

"Hey, I've got an idea. Why don't we get those two honeymooners together instead of prolonging their agony."

Lisa giggled and added softly, "I've got a better idea. Let's watch them. Instead of shutting them off in a room by themselves, let's bring them out here in the living room. We'll dim the lights and . . ."

Simon tried to get up from the depths of the couch and failed as he added, ". . . and turn on the music . . ."

". . . and we'll give them romance by candlelight," she finished with a soft, throaty laugh.

Lisa floated out of the room to get Cushion as Simon screwed himself out of the couch and went around turning out the lights. The FM was tuned to a soft music station from New Jersey as a cool breeze blew through the windows. She returned from her bedroom holding her spaniel by a leash in one hand and balancing a lit candelabrum with the other. She set the silver piece on a plate on the white oval dining table and walked Cushion over to the couch, where she joined Simon. With warm, wet hands, Simon stroked the lovely dog and deliberately unclipped her leash from the collar and in a fluid action commenced to unbuckle the collar itself.

"There," he said in a slow, low voice. "It's all off."

Taking her cue from Simon, Lisa began unbuckling the large, thick metal-studded collar of Toro. In a slow motion, both dogs were free. The handsome couple then sat back against the couch, both with their legs tucked beneath them, and relaxed in anticipation. Cushion walked out in the middle of the carpeted floor and scratched herself from behind. Toro remained at Simon's feet, first looking at the dog and then looking at Simon.

"Go ahead, boy. It's okay. She's waiting for you."

Toro slowly moved from his spot and walked toward the waiting Cushion in well-defined movements. In that moment, Lisa clutched Simon's left thigh with both her hands. With hot darts piercing his body he placed his arm around her shoulder tenderly and gave her a flared nostril. She flared back. Toro stood over the lying Cushion like a gloating Hun and licked his lips. He poked his head beneath her tail and whimpered a muffled cry. Cushion swiftly swayed her tail from side to side and waited for another pass. The big boxer slowly turned, walked back to his master's feet, and slumped down to the floor.

"Hey, what the hell's the matter with you, anyway. Go to it, man. It's there waiting for you. Move. MOVE!"

Lisa removed her hands from Simon and said, "Take it easy. Maybe she just doesn't turn him on or something. Maybe he's sick. Maybe he just doesn't like girls."

The mood changed and Simon blurted out, "What do you mean 'doesn't like girls'? There's nothing wrong with that dog! I wish I had as many women as that dog has had. I'll tell you what's wrong here. You and that stupid feminine spray. Your atomizer. You're not supposed to spray anything into a dog that's going to mate. They like that smell. They need it."

She tugged her dress to her body with a snap and answered, "If you're going to be vulgar, I'd rather you'd leave. LEAVE NOW!"

Simon rubbed his hand against his forehead and made

a desperate attempt to salvage his gurgling biology. "Look, why don't we give them a little more time?" He started to laugh a little as he continued, "We can rub that ridiculous spray deodorant out or wash it out . . ." With each new word he became more involved with stifling his laughter, which was starting to gush out. In an instant he became hysterical, and soon he was laughing uncontrollably. The more he laughed, the angrier Lisa got. She grabbed Toro's leash and collar from the floor and shoved them into Simon's hands. By this time he was in an uncontrollable fit of gagging laughter. She pushed him toward the door. Tears were spilling down his face as he tried hard not to double up. She opened the door and went back for the dog. With a swift boot from behind, she shoved both Toro and his master out into the hallway.

"You're a drag, you know that? And your lousy dog's a complete turn-off. You're both a pair of impotent, celibate, incompetent fumblers. Come back when you've both had a little more experience!" She slammed the door but could still hear the hysterical laughter all the way down the elevator shaft. "Big deal! Who needs it?" she muttered as she snuffed out the candles.

Toro was a normal, healthy dog with no sexual difficulties. The same was true of Cushion. It is a natural part of a dog's life to mate and to reproduce puppies, but every species in nature has been programmed to conform to its own unique set of behavior and circumstances related to sexual activity. So delicate is the process that if any of the conditions necessary are tampered with, the mating will not take place. When inexperienced humans attempt to mate dogs and violate the necessary procedures, not only is there no consummation, but the animals come away frustrated and possibly harmed psychologically.

Clearly, there is much transference of human thought, emotion, and drive involved in sexual liaisons arranged by amateur dog owners. The tendency would seem to be to apply to the dog ideas peculiar only to the needs and appetites of humans. There is little that dogs and humans have in common sexually, and yet the issue is too often forced.

A male dog becomes sexually mature anywhere between six and eighteen months depending on the breed and the individual dog's physiology. The larger the breed, the longer it takes to reach maturity. The American Kennel Club does not register puppies unless both parents were at least one year old when mating. The female is considered mature when she experiences her first estrus cycle, commonly referred to as "heat" or "being in season." Here again the breed and size of the dog affects maturity, which is reached between six and twelve months.

The sexual behavior of wild canids differs greatly from that of their domestic cousins. Wolves and coyotes are essentially monogamous and mate with one female for life. Female wolves experience one estrus cycle a year, while dogs experience two. In an extended pack the leader sometimes will not breed so that he'll have more time to fulfill his responsibilities for pack survival. In such cases, he will leave breeding to lower ranked males.

Because dogs have been domesticated for so many centuries, their sexual behavior varies greatly from the wolf and other wild canids. Feral dogs will breed indiscriminately, but unless a dog has lived in a kennel or pack situation, he has not had the opportunity to learn proper sexual technique through observation. Confinement and close contact with humans have somehow rendered many male house pets hesitant and unassertive in breeding situations. This is not to say that a dog on the loose will not successfully mount a wandering female in heat. Many dogs must be guided and instructed during their first mating. Some domesticated females become frenzied in their first sexual encounter. This is not at all natural to the dog, but is nonetheless common. Timing is also of great importance. If a male is thrust into a situation with a female who is not yet at the receptive moment of estrus, she will behave in a very aggressive manner. This tends to permanently affect the male's attitude toward mating if it is his first experience.

It is customary to bring the female to the male on his home ground. In the wild only the male claims territory. There must be some time allowed for the two animals to become acquainted through the wire of separate kennels, runs, or cages. The male should not be allowed to eat two hours before mating, and both animals must be toileted before being brought together. Noise, audience, afternoon sun, and all forms of distraction must be avoided. Once the animals are introduced to each other they can be left to perform sexually; however, they must be observed to be certain that they have successfully mated. Here the knowledgeable breeder knows that assistance is very often required, and knowing what to do and when to do it is based on knowledge gained from years of experience. Entire books have been written on the subject of breeding dogs. It is not within the purview of this work to adequately explore the subject. It is important to understand the principles of pack behavior when it comes to sex. In a pack, a male is designated as leader because of his size, strength, courage, and ability to lead. He claims territory, finds prey, leads the others in making the kill, selects a mate and propagates. Even the most timid of domestic dogs bases his behavior on these principles. This is especially important when breeding dogs.

When breeding dogs, there is absolutely no value in doing so unless your intention is to produce a dog as good or better than the one which is being bred. The striving for breed perfection is an honorable and worthwhile goal. There can be no other reason that makes sense in a society that can no longer humanely sustain the present pet population.

There are already more dogs than there are homes for them. Breeding puppies for fun or profit is less than useless, it is ignorant and inhumane. If puppies are brought into the world for the benefit of a child's education, what is that child learning if the dogs end up in decompression chambers or out on their own scavenging for food in garbage cans?

Allowing dogs to mate when there is no reason for it other than some hidden significance to the humans involved is mindless. It is quite clear that male dogs do not have to be bred in order to live full and happy lives. It is best never to introduce a male house dog to sex (arranged or otherwise) if he is not to function as a constant stud. The typical dog will not miss what he has never had and will in all probability not experience any frustration. For the male that is constantly mounting human legs, vertical objects, or children, the best and most humane solution is castration. A castrated male dog is a wonderful pet that becomes sharply focused on his human family. It has been the experience of many dog owners that their male house dogs have had certain changes of personality after one or two matings. They can become more dominant, more territorial, less playful, less tolerant. This is not always the case but it remains a possibility and should be considered before allowing a house pet to breed.

The sexuality of the female is much different. Unless she is spayed, whether she likes it or not, she will come into season twice a year and experience a hormonal and chemical change in her body at that time. A female usually experiences her estrus cycle every six months, and it normally lasts a total of twenty-one days. During the first week there is a bloody discharge which becomes somewhat colorless in the second week and disappears during the third and final week. This happens whether the dog is ever mated or not. During the three weeks of estrus, twice a year, it is necessary to sequester the animal so that no males can get at her. The best method is to board her at a kennel. If she is to remain at home, she should be kept under lock and key so that there isn't the remotest chance of her darting away and mating with a neighborhood dog. If the dog is not going to be shown in the ring or bred for puppies, having her spayed between six months and four years of age solves all problems pertaining to sex.

Toro and Cushion may or may not have been meant for each other. But the manner in which they were brought together (not to mention the reasons) made it an impossibility. Unfortunately, they were made to suffer far more from the unsuccessful mating than their frivolous owners.

Cats

There is much that is violent about cat sex. During the time that a female goes into heat, most available males in the area smell and hear her condition. Both local and foreign studs will congregate around the female in an effort to mate with her. Territory is violated, and the rules of social rank are up for grabs. The female, or queen, will remain in her sexually receptive condition for several days and will allow herself to mate with more than one cat during that time. As a matter of fact, she may mate many times with each available male.

While she waits for the right moment, the tomcats gather and eventually fight it out for top-cat position. There is a formal set of behaviorisms connected with a fight of this type. The confronting males arch their backs and raise their fur as they emit the most incredible screeches and growls. They slowly approach each other until finally one springs for the neck of the other. They roll about as they bite and slash at each other. The sound is terrifying. After several awful minutes, they break apart and rest. Very shortly they have another go at it and repeat the same actions. This happens again and again until one cat decides not to return for the next bout. He has signaled his defeat and steps aside for the superior male.

All the while, the female has distracted herself and remained aloof from the confrontation. Once it has been established which tom will be her first mate, a courtship takes place that is also ritualized, almost to the point of choreography. He chases and she moves away. If he does not follow, the queen will stop and entice him with rubbing gestures and rolling on the ground. If he gets too close too soon, she will hiss, spit, and even throw a punch. Finally, when she is ready, she will lower the front of her body and raise her back. In a crouched position, she moves her tail to the side and exposes her genitalia. The male mounts in a furious leap. He will hold her still with a firm biting grip on the back of her neck. This is not meant to hurt, but rather to restrain her. She is then held in position with all of the tom's legs as he quickly inserts his penis into her vulva. There may be several attempts before insertion is accomplished. Ejaculation takes place immediately. The female's instant reaction is a torturous shriek that sets one's blood running in the opposite direction. She then disengages, frees herself from the male grip, strikes him with a slashing claw, and scurries away.

Mating will continue in a short while. The two animals may copulate as many as five or ten times within a thirty-minute period. The mating process can continue for as long as twenty-four hours and longer, depending on how long the female's estrus lasts. During this time, the male may tire of her and allow the others to fulfill the duties of his office. Pregnancy is almost a certainty. Love's labour has definitely not been lost. Although the consummation of cat sex is charged with emotions, it is at its worst when it is thwarted.

Harlow was living proof that not all white cats are deaf. She could hear everything she wanted to hear. She

could almost hear the mental processes in the people that
lived with her as they merely considered if it was meal-
time. Don't misunderstand. There was a ritual connected
with allowing "them" to entice her with food. First, they
had to express sentiments of undying love and devotion.
Next, came a long dirge about how life would have no
value without her. And finally, a few lines of verse or an
occasional madrigal just to get the stomach juices flowing.

She lived in a large pressboard castle, Harlow did. It
was set up for her during her first Christmas with David
and Helen Murray. They spent an hour and a half trying
to interpret the instructions for assembly. When it was
finally completed, the cat moved in immediately and
didn't come out for two days. They had to shove her food
bowl inside and plead with her to eat. But that was many
months ago. Somehow the sultry furess understood that
she was the first cat the Murrays ever had. Perhaps it was
because they tried so hard to please her.

They considered themselves fortunate to have such a
glamorous-looking cat. Like her namesake, Harlow was a
silver-blonde with a coat resembling the movie star's
clingy white satin gowns. All that was missing were the
penciled eyebrows. If there was such a thing as reincarna-
tion, then Jean Harlow had returned to earth in the body
of a gorgeous, slinky white cat with copper-colored eyes.
She was low-down, trashy, and desired by all who saw
her. She should have been in pictures.

David was a dreamer, but Helen was a planner. She
got the two of them organized in quick order and opened
a joint savings account the day after their wedding.
Their honeymoon consisted of one night in a posh hotel
and don't-be-late-for-work-in-the-morning. They were
copywriters and worked in separate ad agencies. Her plan
was to put together enough funds to impress a bank and
borrow financing for their own agency. She figured they
each could swipe some accounts from their respective

employers and have a sufficient client list to survive their first year. They did just that and she was right. They squeaked through their first year and showed a small profit. Things improved in their second year, and from then on they were the proud owners of a going concern and well on their way to prosperity. It was then that Harlow entered their lives.

By her seventh month, Harlow abandoned her castle for a waterbed and a carpeted tree house. If there was a toy or a luxurious convenience, it was snatched from the store and immediately installed in the Murray apartment. She often played with a blue satin ball with a faint bell inside, but was torn between that and her fur-lined mouse. Once David discovered that she enjoyed sleeping under his winter overcoat which he often tossed on the couch, he left it there as a permanent blanket for her highness. It was her favorite napping spot, and she crept into it around seven every morning, just as David and Helen were waking up. They had to lift the collar to say good-bye on their way to work. Harlow never opened her eyes until ten.

By now Harlow, who was seven months old, could no longer be regarded as a kitten. She was a young cat. The Murrays got home late one evening and rushed to prepare dinner. Helen was sautéing onions in butter when a peculiar odor intruded. It was an elusive scent and came and went depending on how close she came to the bubbling pan. She tilted her head and took a good whiff of the onions. They smelled wonderful. She shook her head and went on with her dinner preparations.

David shouted something to her from their bedroom but could not be heard over the sizzling onions. He stuck his head into the kitchen and said, "What is that awful odor? It smells like you're cooking an old foot."

Helen frowned and answered, "You smell it too? I

thought it was the onions, but there's something bad around the house."

Two minds with a single fear, they ran to the bathroom where Harlow's litter box was hidden in a linen closet, behind a partially opened mirrored door. Naturally, it was no ordinary litter box. It was a big, bold blue affair made of molded plastic. It was completely enclosed with a rooftop and circular entrance way. The top half came off when the litter was to be changed. In his effort to undo the stubborn top piece, David jerked the whole container off the floor, spilling much of its contents over his lap and between the fibers of the bathroom carpet. Helen checked the debris as David cleaned up. There was nothing there that could cause so pungent an odor as the one that cut through the onions which by then had begun to burn. For the rest of the evening all they could smell were burnt onions.

The next day came and went and they could clearly detect the same unpleasant odor as soon as they walked through the door. There was no mistaking it now. Something quite bad was in the air. It was hard to tell if it was acrid, rancid, rotten, or raunchy. With zeal and determination, they went from nook to cranny to cubby and could not locate the source of the odor. Helen stopped her search suddenly and shushed David. "Listen."

"What?"

"The bedroom window. Something's at the bedroom window."

They ran into the bedroom and opened the curtains with a quick pull on the drawstring. Standing on the outer ledge of the window was a large, dirty cat. There was some orange and some white and some black on its dingy body. The cat was sitting on the ledge with its back facing the window. Its rear end began to quiver, and the large animal raised its tail and began to squirt onto the glass pane. The discharge seemed somewhat thicker than urine as it hit the window in a steady stream and rolled down onto the ledge. When the cat finished, he turned around to look the Murrays in the eye. Just then another cat hopped up onto the ledge but was knocked down by the already-seated sprayer. Helen was too astonished to do anything, but David hit the glass with his knuckles and scared the big cat away. And then the odor hit. An almost overwhelming smell began to drift into the bedroom and slowly throughout the rest of the apartment. It was quite nasty.

Just then Harlow appeared in the bedroom and in one jump went from the bed to the windowsill, sniffing around where the glass met the wooden frame. There were several cats out in the back courtyard of their building. They began a symphony of *merrowlling* that upset the humans but clearly interested Harlow. David swept the young thing up in his arms and carried her swiftly out of the room. "Don't you listen to them, Harlow. They're just riff-raff." Helen did the best she could to wash down the outside windows, but the smell was impossible to eradicate. She just couldn't understand why the neighborhood toms decided to single them out for this vindictive assault on their peace and tranquillity.

Days went by and the male cats assembled outside their back windows like an orchestra perpetually tuning up and never getting to the composition. The windows were sprayed every night by one or more daring tomcats. David was exasperated, but it was seriously affecting Helen. She was getting a bit hysterical. They tried very hard to shield Harlow from the obscene caterwauling coming from the backyard. Out of sheer desperation, they locked her in the bathroom (with a transistor radio playing Schubert quartets).

Helen had a rock concert in her head and desperately needed some aspirin. She opened the bathroom door, and out scooted Harlow into the bedroom. The cat's behavior was intensely different from anything the Murrays had ever seen her display before. The goddess had lost her cool. She jumped up onto the windowsill and tried to get through the glass with futile clawing gestures. In her frustration, she hopped down and began to roll over and over all the while rubbing her rear end against the freshly laundered chenille bedspread. It was quickly losing its whiteness. "Harlow!" shouted David. "What the hell's the matter with you?"

With a low and painfully loud groan, Harlow began emitting sounds that seemed to indicate surgery without benefit of anesthesia. She rubbed her chin on the carpet as she lifted her hindquarters high in the air. All the while she kept thrashing her hind legs as if wiping them clean against the carpet. From this wholly unattractive position, she would then roll over again and then quite suddenly begin to groom her coat with her tongue. Without stopping, she kept repeating these actions to the accompaniment of her chilling groans which sounded like a cross between a trombone blast and a belch. It went on for a full hour before David could get a veterinarian to answer the phone—much less agree to see the cat at nine o'clock at night. While he was on the phone, Harlow rubbed furiously against his leg as if in terrible pain while Helen tried to keep from having a nervous breakdown in the bathroom. David finally found a veterinarian who would see him. He bundled himself and the cat up and chased a taxi a block and a half before it would stop.

Two hours passed before David entered the door to their apartment. Helen was nervously waiting for him. She was crazed. "Where's Harlow?" she shouted hysterically.

"Take it easy, Helen. She's okay. I left her with the vet."

Helen gulped and sank into the couch unconsciously

stroking the overcoat Harlow usually slept under. "Tell me the truth. I can take it. No, lie to me. I don't want to know. If she's got cancer, I'll die."

David began to laugh as he poured himself a large measure of bourbon. "She's not sick, she's just in love," he hummed. "Our dear little kitten is no longer a kitten. She's a big old cat and has her appetites."

"What are we going to do," asked Helen as relief began to spread over her body.

"It's being done . . . tomorrow," replied David. "As of tomorrow Harlow is a capon. She'll never go through this again. She is being fixed, altered, neutered, el spayola."

Helen began to cry. "Poor Harlow."

David finished his drink, sat down in a chair and looked up at the ceiling. He had a slight smile on his face, not unlike a father whose daughter had just canceled her wedding.

———————◆———————

To the uninitiated, feline sexuality comes as a rude and frightening shock. It creates the impression of horrible pain, emotional trauma, and uncontrollable body misfunction for the cat. The poor loving humans stand by and agonize over their cat's great illness. Although some cats do get hurt in the process, particularly those males that must compete, there is a natural order at work that all felines must conform to—indeed, they cannot avoid it. However, it is of the utmost importance for cat lovers to understand that neither male nor female cats are sick or in pain when they lock into the cyclical compulsions connected with the mating procedure. It only appears that way.

Unlike domestic dogs, domestic female cats will continue to have many cycles of estrus throughout the year, unless they become pregnant. Depending on the ratio of daylight to darkness, domestic female cats can experience periods of heat up to four times a year and maybe more. It is theorized that the pituitary gland is triggered by so many hours of daylight and releases the hormones necessary to change the animal's body chemistry in the complicated process of estrus. In the wild, felids breed but once a year. Domesticity with its environmental and physical alterations of the animal's existence has had a profound influence on this activity. Artificial lighting and other "civilized" factors in the domestic cat's life have surely had their effect.

Male cats will mate at any time of the year if they are stimulated by a female in heat. It has been noted that males living in a state of partial or absolute freedom tend to curb their sexual activity during the colder months of the year. Male cats reach maturity between six and eighteen months, depending on the breed, the individual cat, the climatic conditions of the cat's environment, and the amount of stimulation from other cats.

Harlow was a very normal cat who reached her first estrus at seven months. Although the first stages of estrus were imperceptible to the Murrays, it had not gone unnoticed by the gentlemen cats of the neighborhood. A period of estrus or heat lasts up to three or four days if the female is mated but will continue for ten days if she is not. The sultry white cat had already been in heat for two or three days when the local toms began congregating outside her window. She had been emitting an odor attractive to them, thus letting them know of her presence and physical condition.

The young studs were already in a state of sexual stimulation before they even saw her. Part of the stimulation involved the competition for her favors. Each tomcat sprayed the window and outer walls with his urine, which contains an especially pungent substance designed to mark off the area by scent. This is a form of claiming territory for the benefit of the other male cats and also to communicate with the queen in heat.

When her sexual stimulation began to reach an intense level, Harlow began to vocalize in low and throaty sounds that scared the hell out of her family. These sounds can only be interpreted as a mating call. They are loud and terrifically vibrant. This sound is meant to carry a very great distance so that males in other territories can hear it. In the wild, the female has her own range and territory as well as the male. In order to mate, she must catch the attention of a male who might be as far as 20, 30, 50 or more miles away. It is for this reason that her estrus cycle lasts as long as it does. There would not be much procreation if a male took four days to reach the female and found on his arrival that her needs no longer existed. Once again, nature has not recognized the instant gratification available to dogs and cats living in domesticity. Cats remain genetically programmed for life in the wild state.

Because of this time delay between the onset of estrus and the peak moment of female readiness, stray male cats find themselves gathered in a crowd, waiting. They are neither polite nor quiet. Their very presence is an added factor in intensifying the female's seeming erratic behavior. Eager male cats are a frightening prospect to a female in her first heat. However, as her needs become greater, their presence becomes less fearsome and more desirable. A female in heat will do all in her vocabulary of cajolery to induce her human family into letting her out to meet the gathering toms. She will purr and rub her body against her owner's legs in a back-and-forth motion. She will meeow ever so sweetly and roll around the floor, being as precocious as she knows how. What she really wants is to get at the male cats.

Most kittens are born because of free-roaming cats that are not restrained by the limitations of confinement or sexual altering. Far too few cat owners understand the sexuality of their pets. They inadvertently permit unwanted pregnancies or create tremendous sexual frustration by locking their animals away during periods of sexual need.

There can be no doubt that domestic cats are better off when they are sexually altered. Males should be castrated and females given *ovariohysterectomies* (spayed), provided that the animals are not valuable for breeding purposes. Breeding cats are usually those purebred specimens that have been genetically selected over a period of years for special qualities of physical and mental perfection. These are developed most often by members of the cat fancy who own and operate catteries in a humane and professional manner.

An altered cat will never experience sexual frustration or the rigors of backyard mating. Life is certainly much pleasanter for the humans involved as well. A castrated male cat will not have a need to wander far from home or become involved in many horrible fights resulting in cuts, bruises, or infections. The castrated male will also never spray the walls of his home with the acrid odor of sexually scented urine. Primarily, he will not impregnate a female thus adding to the already-overloaded pet population.

The spayed female will cease to experience the many cycles of estrus throughout the year once she has had her operation. There will be no attractant odors, no radical behavior changes, and no disturbing groans. All activities associated with reproduction will cease. However, the personality of the animal does not change, nor does any other aspect of behavior. And, Harlow will always appear to be someone special to her owners, even if she is no longer a sex goddess.

CHAPTER SEVEN

CATS, KIDS, AND CANINES

Dogs

With a little caution life is not too difficult when a newborn baby enters a home with a resident *best friend*. After proper introductions and a sniff-'n'-see session, simply keep the dog and the infant separated unless someone is in the room monitoring the situation. Even a well-intended dog can injure an infant. If the dog is a decent sort, and most are, he will quickly accept the baby as a new member of the family and become somewhat protective and even responsible for the child's safety. But nothing stays the same, and babies become crawlers, walkers, and runners. Dogs . . . well, dogs just get older.

When a very young child first begins to crawl, the family dog gets a wee bit nervous about it. He doesn't want to hurt the innocent creature, nor does he want his person or his possessions disturbed in any way. An even-tempered animal will do his best to avoid conflict by stepping around the creepy crawler. He might even be amused and accept this new wrinkle as a game in which he can participate. But when the babe dunks a little hand in the dog's water bowl, the dog's only recourse is to shove the child away or look to the adult human for help. With proper supervision, a crawling baby can be encouraged to stay in one or two rooms in which the dog is not allowed, and that will save the day.

Things change slightly once the baby grows into a novice toddler and begins to take those early first steps. The one-year-old wobbles and shakes as it does its own version of the Frankenstein monster. The child begins to sway and reel and then fall flat on its diaper. When a baby first begins to walk, there is little or no physical control over direction or speed. There is only the most fervent desire to propel forward. This then begins to cause trouble for the family canine. If he happens to be in the same room with a baby trying to walk, he cannot be sure where to go that's safe from the little kicks and two-steps. The child comes barreling down the kitchen floor like a little mechanical toy out of control and more than likely will step on the dog's resting snout. Even so, the patient dog, responsible leader that he is, will make every effort to dodge the tiny marcher and find a way to avoid a collision.

Between two and three years, the toddler has mastered the art of walking and is now in great need of moving those legs fast and furiously. There is much energy to be expended. A small living space or a confined child on a rainy day is hellish for a dog just trying to get along.

———◆———

It was an especially sunny day for February. The glaring winter light was melting the icicles off the apartment-house canopy at a steady rate. The sidewalk was sparsely covered with melting slush, the kind that catches in the cuffs of trousers. Too hot for boots, too wet for leather. A fine day for coming home with a new life. The baby was pink, but the cocoon of a blanket was blue and blue satin.

Welcome to the world, Timothy Starn. His dad cried at the moment of his delivery, thus rendering himself useless as a natural-childbirth coach. But Woody did manage to photograph his newborn son anyway. Hilary was forced to do her own counting as she breathed to stay ahead of the painful contractions. It was a normal birth, free of complications, thank God, and both parents were very proud of themselves. They had given up coffee, whisky, cigarettes, aspirin, artificial sweeteners, automobile fumes, and the purple ink stamped on the sides of beef, all to enhance their growing fetus's chances at the moment of retrofire and reentry. Their obstetrician laughed, but the pediatrician thanked them.

The doorman grinned from ear to ear and stole a peak at the blotchy little face sleeping under the bonnet as he let the Starns into the building. The three of them were now an official family unit according to the census takers. The self-service elevator whisked them upstairs quickly to the sixth floor and as a favor did not take its usual circuitous route to the basement laundry-room first. They unlocked the door to their small four-room apartment and damn near slipped on the freshly waxed hardwood floor. Apples had to run for his life because the three of them would have certainly fallen on him. It was a bad sign, but the good-natured dog refused to accept it in that light.

In the parlance of dog lovers, Apples was in the sweetheart category. He was four years old and had lived most of his life with Woodrow and Hilary Starn in their very comfortable apartment. He was born on a farm and was the progeny of a casual mating between a golden retriever and a shepherd-collie. The golden retriever, his mother, had a very nice life on the farm; she was allowed to live in the house even though her job was keeping the horses company.

It was winter when she whelped, and it was a small litter—only three pups. Her family had set up a stall of her own and matted it with over a bale of hay. The temperature had dropped to zero or less and things got terribly cold in the barn. As a result, the proud mother and her litter were taken into the cavernous farmhouse to keep warm. One little puppy had somehow wandered away from the warmth of his mother and couldn't find his way back in his blind puppy state. He started to yipe incessantly and was found in the winter-apple bin. He had splatted over several of the best-looking ones. From then on he became known to the family as Apples. All of the puppies were coddled and played with and thoroughly enjoyed over the long, cold winter months. It was good for them and good for the folks.

Spring arrived late that year and brought with it the Starns, who were trying to make their fantasy come true about a piece of country property. They couldn't come anywhere near the price of the farm, which had just gone on the market, but they did go home with a puppy. Riding in the back seat of their Volvo was the little tyke who resembled a cross between a coyote and an apricot. He was now Apples Starn.

Life in the city was very much to Apples's liking, even if it was different in many ways from the life of his childhood. He never did get to learn much about those huge four-legged critters that his mother fussed with so much. Now and again he had a vague recollection about large expanses of land where a dog could run to his heart's content. Sometimes when the sweet dog was in a very deep sleep, his legs made jerky motions as if they were running. And indeed he probably was somewhere in the purple mist of another world, running through the freshly cut winter grass, trying to catch up with his beautiful mother who was in another pasture, chasing the horses. Whenever he woke from such a dream, he would stroll to his food and water bowls, sniff them just to be sure they were intact, and curl up again between his own Scots plaid blanket and the warm, soft carpet. That was his world and he liked it just fine. The Starns were a nearly perfect couple and loved him like a son. Everything was set up to his liking until that morning when they returned home from the hospital with the newest member of the family.

It took an hour or two for the commotion to settle down once they came in with the little creature who began to scream and howl the moment they entered the apartment. The crying at first frightened Apples, but once he realized there was nothing to fear, he settled down to accepting it as a mere irritant. He patiently waited for his family to stop fussing about with that awful new animal so that they could praise him for something, for anything. He was in desperate need of a good praising and a head rub. After a while he found his hard rubber ball and carried it to Woody in his teeth, and plopped it in his lap. "Geez, not now, Apples. I've got a headache." The orange-blond dog retrieved the ball with his mouth and looked for Hilary. She was moving so fast between the linen closet, the chests, and the storage closets that the dog couldn't even catch her eye, much less her lap. In desperation he hopped up on their night table and deposited the chewed-up ball into the bassinet where the baby was patiently waiting to have his hunger looked after. After the initial shock, the baby looked wide-eyed at the dog face peering in at him and immediately went to sleep. Hilary screamed when she saw the dog leaning on the edge of the bassinet with his two front paws. Woody came running into the room in a mad dash. Apples leaped high in the air and scrambled to the living room, behind the couch where he commenced to pee a quart and a half. He did not come out for the rest of the day.

In the years that followed, Apples made his peace with the child who started out as Baby Starn, progressed to

Timmy, Timothy, and now, almost three years old, Tim.
It's not so much that Tim made Apples crazy as that he
occasionally upset him. A four-room apartment is not an
overwhelming living space. From the very beginning,
Woody was forced out of his den so that it could become
the nursery. He had to sell his old rolltop desk and buy
a Sears mini-size desk for a corner in the living room. It
was there he did such things as work out his income tax
and other paper work that he took home on occasion.
Hilary did her sewing on the kitchen table now, and even
Apples vacated his favorite spot next to the heat pipe in
what was now Tim's room. Everyone had to compromise
and sacrifice for the young master of the house. Apples
tried not to mind.

It's not that Tim didn't love the dog. It's that he had
his needs and the dog had his own. As a matter of fact,
Tim was constantly hugging the beleaguered animal and
making grand statements of his feelings. His favorite activity was sucking the tip of the dog's tail and soaking it
till it dripped with saliva. Apples was constantly moving
his tail away, tucking it under his haunches, and sitting on
it. But the good-hearted dog made a game of it and was
amused at Tim's attempt to grab it during these sessions.
The dog's answer to Tim's learning-to-walk period was to
spend the better part of the waking hours under the
kitchen table. But even there he was subject to Tim's
probes. There was really no place in the small apartment
where the dog could get away from the toddler for very
long. His only defense was when Woody or Hilary stopped
the little boy's affectionate pursuit.

Apples was now seven years old and Tim was about to
turn three. What really began to grate on the dog's nerves
was Tim's need to run and expend energy. On a really
needful day, particularly if he didn't get to go outside,
Tim would grab one of his building blocks and throw it
across the entire length of the living room into his own

room and then rampage across the floor in hot pursuit of the thrown object. This was not very relaxing for the dog. It was the last thing he needed now that he was getting older. At one point he jumped into the air and caught the block with his teeth, ran under the big bed with it, and chewed it to splinters. At first Tim was amused, but his giggling stopped when he saw what had happened to his possession. Then he began to cry. There was a small commotion that ended with Tim going to his room and Apples being locked in the bathroom as punishment. Hilary sat down at the kitchen table over a cup of coffee and a migraine.

Apples was let out of the bathroom that evening when Woody got home. He took the dog out for his walk and stuffed four biscuits in his mouth once they were outdoors. The dog loved them. Woody felt terrible about the incident. He and Hilary loved the dog almost as much as they did Tim. They simply weren't sure where they were all heading.

It rained the next day, and Tim had to play indoors again, much to the misery of Apples. Around eleven in the morning, Tim took the paper hat that his mother made for him and the cardboard sword and decided to play march. With the sword raised high in the air and his hat cocked to one side, he got behind Apples and forced the dog to move ahead of him for fear of being stepped on. After ten minutes, Hilary had to get off the phone and respond to a horrifying shriek coming from Tim. She ran into his room and saw him crying bitterly as Apples cowered in the corner with a guilt-ridden look on his face. His ears were slunk back behind his skull, his tail between his legs as he hugged the wall.

Tim removed his hand from his cheek to show his mother where he had been bitten. It was a neat set of puncture marks caused by the dog's incisors, the row of front teeth. The skin was broken, red and slightly cut.

The boy was not bleeding, but blood was showing from the puncture wounds. What scared Hilary the most was the location of the wound. It was approximately one inch below Tim's left eye. She scooped up the boy in her arms, wrapped him in her coat, and dashed to the emergency room of the nearest hospital.

That night Hilary explained to Woody that Tim had been given a tetanus shot, which he thoroughly hated, and that the wound had been cleaned with an antiseptic. Tim had wanted a bandage, but the doctor stuck a small Band-Aid on his wrist to please him. The little boy went to bed early without eating much dinner. Both Hilary and Woody toyed with their food without finishing. They were extremely upset.

"What'll we do about Tim's birthday party?" asked Hilary.

"Well, we're not going to cancel. We'll just have to board Apples until it's over."

The two of them sat quietly for a while, avoiding the obvious. They watched television for a short while to break the heaviness in the air. Woody ran to the phone and began dialing.

"Who are you calling?" she asked.

"The Parson farm. Maybe they'll take Apples back."

Hilary began to cry and shake her head. Woody hung up the phone and went to his wife to comfort her.

"I got an operator. The number's been disconnected. They must have sold the farm. I guess we'll just have to cope with the problem in some way. Don't worry, honey. Apples isn't going to be thrown away."

The following week, Timothy celebrated his third birthday with a splendid party for him and his friends. Everyone was there except Woody and Apples. They went out for a long walk in the park. It was the least they could do for a three-year-old's birthday party.

Apples was not sent away. That was the least they

could do for a seven-year-old dog who loved them all very much.

----------------◀----------------

It is a very serious matter when a dog takes to biting a small child. It is usually at the point where parents draw the line and rid themselves of the problem by heartlessly ridding themselves of the dog. In almost all cases of this sort, there is no justice for the dog. He is pushed and badgered, and his position is usurped to an unbelievable degree until he has no choice but to start pushing back in order to survive. Unfortunately, his survival is in greater jeopardy when this happens. A dog that loses his home winds up in a poor second home or none at all. He is cut off from the ones he knows and loves and suffers great emotional trauma and worse. Many dogs who lose their homes find themselves in the pound. From there it's a short walk to the decompression chamber where they are killed.

This situation gets to the very heart of the dog's nature, and understanding it is being able to empathize and try to do the correct thing for all concerned. Dogs, like wolves, are animals that live in a pack or communal structure. The pack can be likened to a nation that works together and strives to make life safe and prosperous for all its citizens. But in order to achieve those goals everyone must play a part and serve some function. As I've said, a social order develops, based on strength, courage and leadership abilities. Once the social order is established, the pack goes about the business of defending territory, finding prey animals and securing food by bringing down the strays and dying members of the prey herds. Mating takes place, cubs or puppies are born, and they are raised, fed, and protected. The pack replenishes itself with new, young population . . . life goes on. This all happens within the discipline of rigid social strata. Only when the leader can no longer perform is he deposed and replaced with another, usually younger and stronger. A sick or wounded member of the pack is treated like one that loses its rank. It is either torn to pieces or abandoned for the sake of the survival of all. A wolf pack or wild-dog pack is only as large as the territory that can sustain it. Every member must pull his weight and take his earned place in the social structure.

Despite the fact that domestic dogs have never lived with those conditions under such austere terms, and despite the fact that domesticity has brought them very far from that stark life-style, it is part of their inherited behavior. All dogs have such genetically organized traits and inherit these values and behaviorisms, even the gentlest house pet.

The pet dog uses the human family as a substitute for the pack unit. This is true even if the family consists of one dog and one human. In most cases the dog accepts the subordinate position and the human or humans take the dominant position. It is an interesting phenomenon when the dog takes the dominant role and the human or humans take the subordinate role as was the case with Mortimer. It happens very often in the pet/family configuration. Once the dominant/subordinate figures have been established, it is extremely difficult—if not impossible—to change those positions without great upset or even psychological disturbance to the dog.

In the story about the Starn family, a situation is posed that frequently occurs in families. Apples had been a member of the family for four years, long before a child entered the picture. A pack of three was established. Apples was placed in a subordinate role for many reasons, not the least of which had to do with his size, his effectiveness in tending to matters connected to his own survival, and to his seniority. From Apples's perspective, Woody and Hilary had taken possession of their apartment or territory long before he arrived on the scene. He was low man on the totem pole for a variety of reasons, all of which made perfect sense and were absolutely acceptable. It is the primary reason that dogs live in human society with such great success. However, a new member of the family came to live with them. To Apples, this child was no better than a cub or puppy, and was regarded as such.

Wild dogs and wolves take excellent care of their young. They nurse and wean their puppies. For a long period of time they will bring freshly killed meat to the den, where the hungry cubs eagerly wait for their meal. Once the young are old enough, they are taken on hunting expeditions and literally taught how to track, kill, and feed off prey animals. In the domestic dog's case, the human is the surrogate guardian and performs all these parental services. This is called *epimeletic behavior,* which means the giving of care and attention. Male wolves are as involved in epimeletic behavior as are the females and often take over some of the responsibilities of rearing the young. In a pack society, "aunts" and "uncles" also help in feeding and looking after the cubs.

Even though an order of dominance and subordination begins to develop within the litter itself, it is quite clear that a cub's or puppy's position within the larger pack structure is definitely a subordinate one. No adult dog or wolf would tolerate the least bit of insubordination from a pup without some form of reprimand such as a cuff on the snout or carrying the offender off by the scruff of the neck with the teeth, or even a controlled bite in a tender area.

Not until the dominant wolf is older and weaker does the younger member of the pack get his way. Then an old or sick member of the pack loses his position by a physical challenge which often results in his death. Old or widowed wolves whose teeth are no longer sharp enough to fight or hunt often become "lone wolves" and live away from the pack, eating what they can scavenge from the leftovers. For these reasons, a change of status is much feared.

In the case of the Starn household, Apples was not

threatened when the baby first came home from the hospital. But as the child began to grow (and grow larger than the dog) and gain more status in the family as indicated by his parents, Apples's imprinted behavior came into play. It was the beginning of a challenge to his dominant position over the child, and that became increasingly more of a threat as the little boy grew bigger. Where he was more or less tolerant of the child's physical abuse as a baby, the dog became less and less tolerant from toddlerhood on. Finally, when Tim tried to push him around the floor by marching behind him, the dog made his stand and in an almost reflexive, ritualistic manner met the challenge to his place in the social order. Hence Tim got bitten on the cheek, and nobody understood why. It would be too easy here to say that the dog simply didn't want to be pushed around anymore. The real point is *who is doing the pushing?* Apples might have tolerated this treatment from the adults of the household.

With these factors taken into consideration, it is a simple matter to make those efforts necessary to assure the dog that his position is secure, at least for a while. Once the child's status begins to change, the dog must be gently and gradually introduced to the idea that the youngster will be a dominant figure. This can be accomplished by having the child slowly take over some of the responsibilities for the dog's needs, such as feeding, walking, and even giving refresher sessions of basic obedience commands. If all this is introduced by the other dominant figures, an even-tempered dog will accept it. It is especially important at that time to maintain the same routine of daily events that affects the dog. He must be fed and walked at the same time as usual. More praise, more affection, and more attention than usual is very helpful. There is no reason for the dog to feel challenged if his family is aware of his true nature, and there is definitely no reason for him to lose his home after so many years of loyalty and devotion.

Cats

When writing books and articles on the subject of cats, there are always two extremes that highly subjective writers go for. At one end of the pole are the saccharin peddlers who talk of cats as though they were some form of pixielike adult-child that tiptoe through our lives with a red bow around their necks, squeaking little baby mews and living on jellybeans. At the other end of the pole are the cat-haters who regard them as cold, machinelike, independent snobs that really want no part of human beings and are either cruelly clever or obstinately stupid. It very often turns out that the true cat-hater, the purist, is one that is allergic to them. Unfortunately, these two extreme views are the major influence when it comes to considering cats and children.

We are told that cats are not really good for children, especially young children; that they are too self-centered to relate to an outgoing child. On the other side of the coin, we are told that children are too rough-and-tumble for the fragile, delicate physique of cats and that the poor dears will end up with a twisted tail at best or a broken bone at worst. Some spoilers also indicate that cats are harmful to the children either because they carry some terrible disease or because they might violently slash them with claws as they slather from their mean mouths. To those who are conversant with children and cats, this is pure kitty litter.

There are diseases that humans can contract from cats, from rabies to ringworm. But let's look at the record and discover how rarely that ever happens. Children catch more colds, flus, viruses, parasites, infections, and other serious illnesses from each other than they do from animals. It is a plain, unvarnished fact. And yet nobody would dare suggest that children give up other children. With the exception of allergies involving animal hair and dander, there is no supportable argument for separating children from their pets, especially if they are fortunate enough to live with cats.

Naturally, cats, like children, require a goodly amount of hygienic care and effort if they are to stay disease-free, healthy, normal house pets. As for cats harming children, it is no more true than any other person or object. A cat starts out neutral. How it is related to is what determines the outcome. A hardback edition of Mother Goose can either be an uplifting, educational experience for a child, or it can be used by one child to bop another on the head. Normal, healthy cats will respond to good care, gentle treatment, affection, and companionship with their own special versions of those good things. But all creatures must be permitted to respond in those terms that are unique to their natures.

The Edmund Kean was a medium-sized theater in the heart of Broadway and was very rarely dark. Because of its Old World comfort, it was much sought after. Its most recent tenant was a drama entitled *The Lean and Hungry Look*, which had sixteen characters, a large cast for a straight play. One of the featured players was a tall, handsome chap named Merrill Saunders.

Saunders was having a long and profitable career, with more money and work than he ever thought he would have. That may have been part of the reasons for the failure of his marriage of ten years. He had met his wife at a summer theater where she was an apprentice actress. Ann Hegge had finished her first year in college and wanted to live in New York and pursue an acting career. Like so many before her, it was a frightening prospect to just leave home and take on the responsibility for her own life. She never really did. That one summer in Maine changed everything. Merrill took her breath away and married her on the last day of the season. The couple set up an apartment in New York and were very happy.

In their second year together, they became parents and added the name Melissa to their annual Christmas cards. She was a very noisy baby who cried and screamed incessantly for the first three months of her life. During that period, Merrill began leaving their apartment late at night to get away from the nerve-wracking howls of the new baby. He proclaimed his need for peace and quiet so that he could go to work the next day with a clear head. His need became a liberty for the taking—and then just a habit. Ann became very involved with her daughter and lost all interest in the theater. By that time, Merrill was getting offers to work on an occasional TV film, but it involved extended trips to California or wherever the film was being shot. He once was away for seven months, working on a feature film in Tunisia.

Over the years, Merrill and Ann drifted very far apart and headed inevitably to a quiet, unemotional divorce with a civilized division of property and responsibility.

Melissa adored her father, and he loved her as much as he was capable. Working as an actor was more important to him than anything else he could think of, including his daughter. Like a bad-tasting cough medicine, Melissa accepted that knowledge and chased after him anyway. Whenever she was free and if her mother permitted, Merrill would spend an afternoon with her. It was usually at some museum where he loaded her up with expensive books brimming over with color plates of paintings and objets d'art and a small bronze bust of Cro-Magnon Man, or something similar. He never invited her to see him in a play and certainly never took her backstage at a theater or film studio. It was an unwritten law that his family was to be maintained in a separate world from his professional life. When Melissa asked to go to the theater and he turned her down, it upset her a great deal. After a while she stopped asking, but it still upset her.

Melissa was referred to by her teachers as a bright, handsome (but not beautiful) child. She was well behaved and very quiet. She did not have any true friends, but few seven-year-olds do. It made things all the more difficult when her mother became sick. There was no one to turn to but her father, and it scared her.

At first she was looked after by a housekeeper and she went to visit her mother at the hospital twice a week. After four weeks, her father came to see her and announced that she was going to move in with him for a while. He explained that her mother would be in the hospital for an indefinite time and that she would not be able to visit her at all. With great apprehension, Melissa asked him, "Are you sure you want me? I've never seen where you live."

Merrill was not insensitive to his child. He knew he was a failure as a father and had let his daughter down many times. He looked down at Melissa's face and rubbed his palm over her smooth, soft cheek and said, "Yes, I want you. I'm sure." He picked up her large trunk by the handle and held her hand as they left the empty home where she had grown up. Melissa had a heart-pounding notion that she'd probably never be coming back to the only place she had ever lived. Although she dared not say it, she had the same notion about her mother.

School had recessed for spring vacation and Merrill had his young daughter on his hands. After the second day she got up the courage to tell her father that she didn't want to go to any more museums. "Okay, okay. What do you want to do?"

She almost blushed when she confessed, "I want to go to the theater and see you act."

He had been to the hospital that day and seen how ill her mother was and he didn't have the heart to turn his daughter down for anything. That night Melissa saw her father on stage for the first time in her life. It was a revelation. He was a total stranger both on- and offstage. The smell of his makeup and the look of his costume made him a different human being, someone she had never known or met before.

As a concession to her, he made up and dressed an hour earlier so that she could see him as he would appear on stage and yet have his customary forty minutes to concentrate on preparing the inner workings of the character he played. Although he would hurt and disappoint her many times in the future, his generosity that night gave her the emotional sustenance from which to draw forgiveness, toleration, and something like love. His unwitting investment that evening would pay him back with the often-tested loyalty of a daughter who loved him.

It was the most exciting night of Melissa's life to see her father transform before her eyes from humdrum museum addict to an explosive colonel in the army of the czar. She respected his orders not to distract him during the intermissions. He explained that he was still working on the character during the breaks and didn't want to lose it. It was a whole new world and seemed bright and exciting. She wandered through the lobby looking at the audience as they chattered about the play, who was there that night, and about each other.

Just as the house lights were beginning to fade, a tiger-striped house cat jumped out onto the stage and in a frenzy chased a moth back into the wings. The audience applauded, the theater turned to black, and the curtain came up. Applause for the set.

Because he didn't know what to do with her, Merrill began bringing Melissa to the theater every night and every matinee performance, which was twice a week. The spring vacation lasted three weeks, and the girl needed to be looked after. Having seen the play from three or four vantage points, Melissa began to tire of the experience. She became restless and somewhat lonely. She missed her mother terribly, but never complained or spoke of it to anyone. One evening, when her feeling of isolation became overpowering, she violated her father's rule and burst into his dressing room during the second intermission. She was about to apologize and grab a much-needed hug but she stopped in her tracks. One of the actresses had gotten there first and was caught in a bear hug of an embrace. She was wearing only part of her costume.

They never even realized that she had come and gone. Melissa quickly closed the door with a discreet efficiency found only among the best servants in the world. Her little chest hurt from the emotional constriction she felt so intensely. While wandering backstage she noticed behind the ropes and the pulleys and dollies there was an old peach-colored divan with satin stripes. It was dusty and covered with several empty hatboxes. She could hear the audience applaud and saw slight cracks of stage lights come in from the bottom of the stacked scenery and hanging curtains.

Very quietly, Melissa removed the hatboxes and lay down on the old but elegant prop. The tears ran, and she fell asleep with tightly pursed lips. She woke from her doze five minutes later and discovered that the tiger-striped cat she saw out on the stage the week before had curled up in front of her and was fast asleep. The cat had propped its head on her stomach and slept in deep and affectionate innocence. At first she was startled but then smiled at her new acquaintance. She patted and stroked the small animal and became intrigued with its undulating response to the smooth delivery of her petting.

When Melissa heard the applause begin for the final line of the play, she automatically grabbed the cat, arose from the couch and headed for her father's dressing room. The pain in her chest had faded, and she became determined to get there before the actress did. The cat made a meeowing sound. She stopped and looked at it. He licked her hand and made himself more comfortable. Melissa gave him a large, uninhibited hug and kiss. "Well, Colonel," she said to the cat, "I think you'd better come home with me. This theater is no place for you. I'm gonna get you a nice bed and a good dinner, and tomorrow we'll see a cat doctor . . ." Merrill wasn't thrilled at the prospect of living with a cat, but it did seem to be important to his daughter, and he wasn't about to refuse her a thing—not for a while, anyway.

During the course of childhood there are many transitional periods of growth and development. Each new phase is fraught with a fear of the new way of being and a refusal to give up the old way. Trading off the security of dependency for the unknown factors of independence creates stormy emotions and a great ambivalence. This is true for every child and is experienced to a much greater degree of intensity by the child caught in the circumstances of tragedy and loss. Every child needs a friend who will remain constant and loyal without qualifying the relationship in any way. This friend must not exact any price in exchange for solace and comfort. Where can one turn for such altruistic behavior? To a pet, of course.

Cats are not psychic, although they certainly appear to be. Most cat owners have a wonderful story to tell about how their pet came to them at the darkest hour and made life seem a lot better than it was at that moment. What is it, one asks, that gives cats the superb sense of timing they have when involved in human events? And what is it about cats that creates the magical chemistry that exists between them and children?

Once we get past the false notion that cats are not as good for children as dogs, it is not too difficult to understand that chemistry. The domestic cat is a vulnerable creature with all of the anxieties of a wild animal but only a few of the physical defenses. Consequently, it responds instantly to gentleness and tender feelings. It does not require ESP for a cat to discern an affectionate, kindly human who has no desire to harm it. When not overly influenced by harsh environmental elements, most children have tender feelings toward other living beings and automatically reach out to pet an animal. (Children have to be taught to dislike snakes or insects, for example.) Their natural inclination is to express respect, love, and curiosity. Normal cats understand normal children on a direct emotional level.

When comparing them to their wild cousins, it is hard to find a parallel to the domestic cat's sweet and loving behavior. One must look carefully to find it. Why do domestic cats develop such warm and gregarious relationships with one or more humans when it never happens in the wild, especially between such felids as lions and cheetahs? There is an answer.

Examine the circumstances of a house cat's life. From kittenhood to death she is cared for like a baby. She is fed, bathed (hopefully), brushed, doctored, played with, and given a fair amount of physical contact expressing acceptance and affection. The identical services are performed in the wild for all felids when they are cubs. These functions are performed by their mothers.

When a lion or tiger cub sets out to investigate the world, it seeks adventure or the gratification of its curiosity. It hasn't the slightest intention of hurting one living thing, and indeed it does not. It haphazardly approaches all things that move and falls back in incredulity when it is rejected. Although an adult domestic cat is somewhat more cautious, it is unbelievably curious and sometimes fearless in its investigations. Domestic cats seem to express disbelief when their advances are rebuffed.

There are many similarities between the wild felid cub and the domestic cat, whether it be a kitten or adult. Although the constant state of play between a human and a cat has its influence, it would seem that the constant state of dependency is what tends to promote a childlike or adolescent set of behaviorisms in the domestic cat. Compare the behavior of a castrated male cat living the life of a house pet with that of a whole tom fending for himself in the back alleys of the city. You'll not find a meditator or Dutch uncle in the city streets. You wouldn't want that tomcat jumping into your child's lap.

Unless a domestic cat is allowed to turn wild the many generations of domestication have had a profound genetic influence on its behavior. Domestic cats (and probably dogs, too) never seem to reach adulthood, which is why we can live with them so successfully. For reasons unknown, cats have the unique ability to adapt to a natural setting and fend for themselves within their physical limitations. Most dogs do not have this ability.

It is a fair assumption that the common bond between a pet cat and a child is childhood itself. For all of their lives, cats need to be cared for if they are to live in the society of humans. For all of their childhood, children have the identical needs. It may be an emotional recognition of this mutual need that allows cats and kids to get together. But the most important aspect of their bond is the good effect they have on each other.

Obviously, a very young child must be taught how to handle a cat so that neither one will be hurt. When a toddler grabs a cat by the hind leg and twists, it's a certainty that he or she will be scratched sharply on the hand or face. Babies and toddlers have much to learn about human relations, much less animal relations. Many a father has had his eye blackened or his glasses broken from the tough swing of a tiny fist. It's not difficult to teach a baby how to behave gently with a dog or cat. The primary factor is learning respect, sensitivity, and compassion from the adult example. A small hand is easily taught how to pet a cat if the word "gentle" accompanies the action. Usually the baby squeals with delight at the luxurious feel of the fur.

Children past four have an affinity for cats that they do not necessarily have for dogs. They are not overwhelmed with bigness or exuberance and find the delicate movements of a cat less frightening and far more manageable. The somewhat independent air (a pose?) of a cat makes them more appealing to a child. It is a far greater reward when they've earned the cat's trust and she feels safe enough to get close.

Cats do like children and respond to their more somber moods. It is a lucky child that has a pet cat during those times when life is difficult and the world is not a pleasant place to be. When a child is confused and troubled, her cat will always be there to offer a bit of warmth and friendship, consistency, and unquestioned loyalty. Surely that compensates for not retrieving a thrown stick.

Cats love to be loved, held, petted, and related to on an emotional level. There may be nothing more pleasant for a cat than a needful child. Of course, this tends to spoil the cat's public image as an independent loner, sophisticated and greedy for privacy. But any sensitive nine-year-old knows the secret of the cat's mysterious ways. It takes one to know one.

CHAPTER EIGHT

ANIMAL CRACKERS
(Pets and Neuroses)

Dogs

Some dogs are nuts. They wheeze their psychosomatic hacks and coughs until they get you exactly where they want you. Others howl, bark, or snarl until you toss them the boneless sirloin or the strawberry parfait. There are the pacers and the chasers, the snappers and the crappers, and the barkers, biters, and quakers. There are those who run from thunder, attack strangers, quiver in traffic, nasty up the sheets, develop sexual attachments to human beings, and eat grass only to throw it up all over the azaleas. Dogs so inclined are often labeled neurotic, depending on how entrenched they have become in their unusual behavior.

Because of the complexity of the human brain and accompanying emotional system, fine lines of distinction must be drawn between psychoneurotic, eccentric, and individualistic behavior among this higher order of mammalia. Human neurosis may be characterized as a disorder of the personality in which behavior is defensive and often exaggerated. The neurotic person experiences anxiety because of unconscious efforts to solve unconscious conflicts. This may manifest itself in loss of memory, obsessions, compul-

162

sions, hysteria, phobias, imagined (or real) illnesses, and, worst of all, depression. Millions of people throughout the world suffer from various forms of psychoneuroses but somehow manage to live with them. Neurosis takes its worst toll when the victim is no longer using these behaviorisms as a defensive measure but has, over the course of time, developed them into an implacable life-style. Clearly, abnormal behavior is far more complicated in human beings than it is in animals. Merely defining abnormal human behavior has become as difficult as treating it therapeutically.

In the most fundamental and general terms, it is possible that humans and animals may share the same set of behavior mechanisms that, when disturbed, create anxiety accompanied by abnormal or neurotic behavior. These fundamental disturbances may be related to territory, social structure, and population density. All creatures vary from individual to individual, let alone among species, order, class, and phylum. However, at some level, they appear to be influenced by the same precipitous circumstances.

Subtlety and imagination make human neurosis enigmatic and elusive. Canine behavior is exquisitely clear in its normal state and equally clear in its abnormal or neurotic composition. Canine neurosis can be so clear that you often step in it. The question is: is the behavior as neurotic as it seems?

———————◆———————

The only one who never felt pain between Siegfried's teeth was Whiskers, a black cat with white paws. The German shepherd often carried the cat in its mouth from one place to another without causing the slightest wince or whimper. As a matter of fact, the affectionate cat loved the ride and thanked her four-legged bus with a tap of her claws on his snout. It didn't hurt the big dog, and he accepted the cuff with gentlemanly tolerance. The cat often played with Siegfried by lying on her back and boxing with his snout as he sniffed her and rolled her about with his nose. He was stoic about her claws and took what came with dignity and gentleness. The black and tan shepherd accepted responsibility and was comfortable with decision making. Siegfried was the head of the house and ran things with efficient authority. His mistress approved because they lived in a high-crime-rate neighborhood.

It was one of those attractive four-room apartments that Marilyn Hill paid for with more than one-fourth of her monthly salary. It was really more than she could afford, but it made her feel successful and somewhat glamorous. Her pale blue wall-to-wall carpet and white telephone with gold bands around the receiver impressed her friends. Her twice-weekly maid service impressed her mother. And the automatic washer and dryer impressed her dates (because they could shower and wash their underwear). Inside her leather hassock, which was a hollow storage bin, she had stored every copy of *Cosmo* since 1974. Scotch-taped on the inside of her louvered closet door was a headline from a clipping: "CHUNKY IS BEAUTIFUL—IF YOU KNOW HOW TO WORK IT!"

The tenant Hill had to promise her mother that she would buy a large dog before moving from the parental home in Chester, Pennsylvania, without being disowned. She was a secretary in a large corporation that moved its headquarters to New York City, offering her the position of assistant head purchasing agent if she moved with them. She took the big step, rented her luxury apartment on the East Side, and acquired the largest German shepherd west of the Rhine. Siegfried was a fancy import and had the papers to prove it. He was too large to compete in the show ring and too easygoing for attack work. He was a steal at $900. The large dog-presence pleased Marilyn's mother even though he was not particularly thrilled with her. He would sulk around the nervous, jerky movements of Mrs. Hill and try not to stare at her. It made her uneasy and kept her visits down to one or two a year. Siegfried was pure gold and his mistress adored him.

Whiskers was two years old and Siegfried was three-and-a-half. In the three years that Marilyn lived in her apartment, she never once had a problem with burglary, molestation, or mugging. Siegfried's presence was well known to the neighborhood by his deep, throaty woof that sent chills down the spines of strangers as they passed the apartment door just a little too close for his pleasure. A single woman, alone, had little to fear with ninety-five pounds of furry guardian sleeping atop her bed every night. The slightest indication of an alien presence in the powder-blue apartment set the dog in motion. When Siegfried stirred, the cat leaped from the pillow to the highest surface in the bedroom, always to the top of the chiffonier. The gentle, sweet, and loving Siegfried was transformed into a medieval beast, barking and slathering to get at the source of the extraterritorial suspect. Only the froth and the spikes were missing. It always scared the hell out of mistress Hill, but she faithfully rewarded him with a loving pat after ordering him away from the door or window or bathroom drip. It was not difficult for her to fall back into her pillow and drift away quickly with a safe smile that bordered just a little on arrogance.

Siegfried was no pussycat. He guarded his lady lovingly, completely. Marilyn was ostensibly the head of the household, but the great Siegfried was its Praetorian Guard. He was king of the hill.

In the years that Siegfried, Whiskers, and Marilyn lived together, life settled down to a very comfortable family style of existence. The relationships developed fully and completely. Each member of the family behaved in a predictable manner to the others, and there was a desirable acceptance and safety in the knowledge of such intimacy. Marilyn did not like strangers knocking at her door, and Siegfried took care of her discomfort. Siegfried did not like being alone, especially during working hours, and Whiskers was the solution for that problem. Whiskers —well, Whiskers just enjoyed her life with the other two and seemed to make the entire household revolve around her. In their own special way, they, too, were a nuclear family. Oh, brave new world!

Nothing could be more important to any dog, especially a dog of Siegfried's age, than predictable consistency and orderly routine. Marilyn hopped out of bed every working day at 6:45, showered, prepared her breakfast, and spent many puzzling hours in front of her bedroom mirror—the one with all the lights that hurt the dog's eyes if he stared into it for longer than a minute. During the hair and face ritual, the dog sat like a sphinx, panting, with his long tongue hanging out one side of his mouth. Whenever some portion of the procedure failed, Marilyn would yell some four-letter expletive and Siegfried would tuck in his tongue, quickly glance at her, and then look away with wrinkled eyebrows (if it can be said that dogs have eyebrows). Her pain was his pain. Her joy was his joy. There was then the quick shuffle at her closet, and out the door. Whenever she left, his heart always sank just a bit. It was like the room's going dark. Poor Siegfried had great difficulty separating his existence from Marilyn's. It was as if they were the same person. However, before he could sink into a drooping state of nonexistence, Whiskers would make a diving attack on his back from some secret perch and cause the dog to forget his bad feeling.

At 6:00 every evening, the two playmates would hear the key going into the lock, and their ears would prick and their hearts would beat faster as all tongue and breathing activities were arrested. In some mental body-clock, Siegfried's concept of his life had to do with splitting apart and coming together again every sixteen hours. He even understood holidays, weekends, vacations, and an occasional overnight visitor. What was hard for him were those rare, now-and-again nights when his mistress did not come home until the morning. And lately it was happening with a disturbing frequency.

On those nights, Marilyn came home from work at 6:00 as always. She fed the animals and took Siegfried on his walk far earlier than usual. Then there would be a frenzy in the bathroom, yet another one of those awful sessions in front of the bedroom mirror, and finally the ordeal at the closet. The doorbell would ring, the dog's hackles would rise as he attacked the door with horrifying fury, and Marilyn would have to command him to retreat. With restless obedience he would sit in the background as a strange man entered the apartment and embraced the attractive young woman.

The first time it happened, the dog sprung into action and would have done severe damage if his mistress hadn't interceded in time with a loud, shrieking "No!" With hurt and confusion, Siegfried slowly loped into the bedroom and slumped to the floor behind the bed. The door slammed and he didn't see Marilyn until the next morning, when she made a mad dash to dress for work. That night, life returned to normal. However, once or twice a week, the routine was interrupted with the strange man's presence, which meant that the animals would not see their loving mistress until the next morning—and at that for only fifteen minutes. Life was getting hard. Siegfried was getting heartsore.

It's not as though Marilyn had ignored or forgotten her responsibilities toward the animals. As a matter of fact, one could say they were still receiving the best of care. Life had taken a turn for the vital young woman, and things were changing or, at least were in a state of transition. Marilyn was too busy, too involved, too intoxicated with her newfound relationship to fully appreciate that things were quickly evolving into another way of living. Although she was not one to fantasize about true romance, love and marriage or any other pulp fiction about men and women, things were happening, be it chemistry, genetic counseling, the Freudian imperative, natural selection, or inner tennis. Marilyn Hill had a feller, and she liked it fine. The thing about it was that there was no way to explain to the dog that she was having one hell of a good time and didn't want it to stop. The truth of the matter was that it never occurred to her that the dog and the cat were a factor in all this.

Harold Eber was a better-than-average man and a good match for Marilyn. He was the sole proprietor of a small camera shop in Manhattan and a better-than-average photographer. Without deprecation, he referred to himself as an artistic merchant and was proud of the self-anointed designation. Between picture sessions, lab work, and over-the-counter sales, he made a decent living but was practical enough to be grateful for Marilyn's position and the income derived from it.

And so a wedding took place, after which Harold moved into the pale-blue apartment. On moving-in day, Siegfried silently watched Harold lug carton after carton through the front door. He grunted and moaned as Harold dragged in leather suitcases, quadraphonic equipment, house plants, campaign chairs, a framed diploma, a color TV, and a handball trophy. He was definitely a substantial presence. Whiskers hid behind the bathtub. Siegfried did nothing but watch from a corner of the bedroom. He had already been introduced to the man and given him tacit approval. Actually, it was more like temporary permission to come in. The new member of the family had no idea that he was there on a temporary visa and that Siegfried had a wait-and-see attitude. He also didn't understand that there were several codicils to this new social contract, and his was a limited partnership from the dog's point of view.

Like all wedding days, even one that involved moving, it came to an end and proceeded toward dinner and then bed. Throughout the evening, a warm glow permeated the apartment, and the family of four seemed to enjoy the occasion. Harold and Siegfried played stick for a while and spent a pleasant fifteen minutes together. All seemed well with the world.

Wineglasses were drained, the dessert remained in the refrigerator, unopened, and the newlyweds prepared for bed. Harold wore his silk pajamas. Marilyn was already under the blankets. Before Harold could move out of the bathroom doorway, Siegfried trotted in from the living room and hopped onto the foot of the bed and curled up as usual. The dog had gone to work for the night as he always had. The honeymooners laughed. Marilyn tried to shoo the big galumph off the bed, but he would not move. The dog stretched out and rubbed his head against Marilyn's knees. She blushed and Harold gulped with something between embarrassment and jealousy. He suggested that they try to ignore the dog for a while.

As Harold came to the edge of the bed, Siegfried uncurled his massive body and sprang to all fours. The dog didn't exactly snarl, but he didn't look any too friendly, either. He angled himself between Marilyn and Harold whenever the anxious groom tried to get into the bed. It soon became clear that Siegfried wasn't about to let him enter the bridal bed. The situation continued unchanged for thirty minutes. The air was tense and anxiety-ridden. It was a standoff.

Marilyn commanded the dog to leave the bed, but the mighty defender paid no heed as long as Harold remained in the room. It was reminiscent of King Kong hanging onto the building with one hand and fighting off the gnat-like airplanes with the other. From a special frame of reference, it was romantic and quite touching. From another perspective, it was terrifying, frustrating, and inevitable, taking into consideration the circumstances of the past three years.

Harold finally moved into the living room to claim the sofa. Marilyn soon followed with sheets, pillows, and blankets. They tried to salvage the evening by telling themselves that they had the makings of a good Broadway comedy in this. They closed the bedroom door, leaving Siegfried alone in the bed to contend with his madness by himself. Harold started to clown around as his bride made up the sofa with the sheets. He grabbed her and fell to the carpet in an embrace just about the same moment that Siegfried began to howl. It was a soulful sound which at first sounded like a distant coyote, but grew louder and more urgent, like a neighborhood werewolf. The amorous couple sighed, released each other, and got up from the floor. The honeymoon was over.

Is a dog neurotic if he obeys every impulse that is true to his nature when confronted with a set of circumstances that parallel a similar situation in the wild? We could say that Siegfried's behavior was neurotic because his defense mechanisms were uncalled for. He was in no apparent danger, even though he acted as if he were. He had been encouraged to defend his mistress from those outside their family circle and to regard his territory as inviolate. Once a dog has been taught these things, once a routine has been established, once a reward system has been set up for the performance of certain duties, it is unreasonable to expect a dog to behave differently just because the circumstances have changed.

All dogs have been genetically organized to behave in certain ways under certain conditions. Again, a male dog with leadership quality will be instinctively drawn to a group resembling a pack. He will develop a territory, establish his status within the pack, defend his territory, defend his status (to the death, in some cases). This is normal behavior for all canids. Why, then, should some dogs behave in what seems to be an irrational manner as did Siegfried?

When we look at a dog barking uncontrollably or behaving in an unnatural manner, it is most certainly an animal under stress. The body of the animal has been prepared for some form of action and will either fight or take flight. The body has precipitated the proper chemical changes so that the order of priorities change. The heart pumps faster, the blood pressure rises sending oxygen to the skeletal muscle instead of the skin, the intestinal system, and the kidneys. If stress continues, the physiology of the animal's body is harmed. When the condition is prolonged excessively or is triggered frequently, the animal will eventually collapse or even die. Violations of the animals needs will cause stress, which in turn will either exacerbate the situation or add new and even more extreme behavior.

Siegfried behaved exactly as he was genetically organized to behave. His training and encouragement went hand-in-glove with his natural inclinations. For three years Marilyn Hill placed him in charge of defending a well-established territory and socially organized pack (or family). His position and duties were absolutely clear. He barked and attacked all intruders as soon as he discerned a threat. He was rewarded with approval and affection for his behavior. He slept atop the bed at the foot and considered that area his nighttime lair. It is little wonder then that he refused entry of this interloper into the inner sanctum of the Hill family.

Three primary elements were brought into play. Harold Eber represented a new and consequently threatening difference in the population density, a violator of the dog's territory, and, most important, an impending threat to the well-established social order of rank. A dog or wolf that has held leader status will not tolerate a challenge to that position without putting up a great struggle. It is a matter of dominance and subordination. Changes in any animal's environment create apprehension, fear, and anxiety, which eventually lead to physical stress. Many so-called neurotic behaviorisms in dogs are a result of fear-provoking changes in the environment such as noise levels, unusual weather, harassment of all sorts, additional population, territory violations, and changes in pack structure.

It is quite clear that Siegfried's refusal to allow Harold entry to the bed was not based on some human emotion such as jealousy or from some unnatural sexual attraction to Marilyn. The dog was simply doing his job as usual. Nobody explained the change to him or took his possible reaction into account. Similar problems often occur in a parallel human situation, and the adults go into shock when the children refuse to accept a new member of the family. Stepparents and newborn siblings often have a hard road to hoe.

Siegfried should have been introduced to Harold on a subordinate/dominant basis. Over a long period of time, Harold could have behaved in a dominant manner with the dog by placing his leash on his collar and taking him for walks, giving him practice obedience commands, feeding him, grooming him, and all the other activities connected with his needs. If the dog had been obedience trained, Harold could have run him through his paces at every opportunity with gentle authority. A relationship would have developed with the dog eventually regarding Harold as member of the pack structure who is higher up on the social scale.

When it was first decided that Harold would be moving in, Siegfried should have been ordered off the bed and given a new sleeping, guarding position in the living room. A large basket, box, or blanket could have been made available as a new lair or private territory. Once the dog accepted this change, Harold's entry into the household would have

been somewhat easier for all concerned. The changes in Siegfried's life-style should have begun long before Harold
moved in and therefore not been associated with his presence. A dog makes no distinction between the demands of a
changed domestic situation and his instincts. It is the business of the dog owner to manipulate the environment so
that the dog can be himself without having to lose his home.
Siegfried's refusal to allow Harold into the bed was irrational but not necessarily neurotic. However, had he been
punished for his behavior, he might have become irre-
trievably neurotic.

Poor Harold was forced to sleep in the living room
until a professional trainer was able to work with both of
them. The technique was to run man and dog through an
accelerated basic obedience course so that Siegfried became
conditioned to accepting Harold as a dominant figure. At
the same time, the trainer corrected the dog every time he
attempted to get up on the bed. After each correction, the
dog was walked to his new sleeping quarters, given praise,
and commanded, "Stay." This all took time and patience.

When you are confronted with abnormal behavior in
dogs, look for its cause. It is usually connected with some
change in the animal's environment that violates his needs
or natural instincts causing fear or anxiety. Correcting the
environmental factor is the primary step toward cure. Patience, affection, and gentle behavior modification are the
best techniques for effecting change. Sometimes a basic
obedience course is the best answer.

Cats

There are many cat owners who do not believe in confining their pets. These are often unneutered lotharios that
run in and out of their homes at will. They exist in the city
as well as the suburbs and rural areas. Sooner or later, free-
roaming cats disappear, causing much worry and heartache

for the humans left behind. With few exceptions, they eventually return, but not without leaving behind a wake of human anxiety. Nothing is more horrible for a pet owner than to have the animal do a disappearing act. The imagination takes over, and the cat is thought to be dead in traffic, mortally wounded in a territory dispute, treed by dogs, cornered by squirrels, or any number of threatening situations causing the heart to skip a few beats. The truth, of course, is that any one of these imagined terrors is possible for a cat with walking papers. The cat that does not come home has probably not been victimized by the vicissitudes of the urban jungle but has found something that has caught his fancy. The cat will linger with some new source of pleasure or interest that he is not ready to give up for the usual dish of kibble and the same chuck under the chin.

If a cat is allowed too much freedom and wanders away he or she is not abnormal, even if he or she stays away for several days or several weeks. Cats that are not restrained may very well be inclined to do this without being considered neurotic, unhappy, fed up, or displeased with the service.

Although you may feel relieved to see the old puss nonchalantly stroll back into the homestead, you must not be astounded that he returned after being gone for so many days. Be astounded if the cat does not return. And how do we explain this strange and mysterious behavior? Do not call it neurosis, call it style.

———————◆———————

Faye Jackson's cat was a beauty. He was long, lean, and muscular, the proud possessor of a shiny gray coat with white paws and yellow eyes. She called him Charles, and he knew enough to come running when he heard that name. It meant some good thing to eat or experience such as a neck rub or a body scratch. Charles was a Greenwich

Village cat and spent most of his time on the rear fire escape of a six-story tenement building. Charles was a virile, male cat—a tom, if you will. Faye liked it that way. She thought it spoke well of her attitude about nature and, in some unique way, ecology.

Charles's manner was more than aloof. He had a dominant attitude associated with an animal that carved out territory, established high rank in the neighborhood, and had all the females he wanted. With a high, vertical tail, he always strutted across Faye's living-room floor like John Wayne on his way to clean out a saloon. Charles was a ballsy cat and lived life pretty much on his own terms.

Every morning before leaving for work, his mistress opened the window leading out onto the fire escape and watched him hop out. She enjoyed thinking about his freedom and often daydreamed at her job about what her perfect Charles was up to at that time of day. He always waited for her at the same window when she came home from work, and it was one of her very pleasant chores to let him in and ask him what he had accomplished that day. She never really got to know, and her confidence in him was such that it never occurred to her that he might have killed another cat or brought more unwanted kittens into the world.

Faye Jackson lived alone and liked it that way. She had been married once but left the man after the second year. After years of dating and enduring the matchmaking efforts of her friends, she settled for a cat. It was better than volunteer work. She acquired Charles from the neighborhood "cat lady" who had devoted her life to rescuing and placing orphaned cats in good homes. Faye never really knew who she was or where she got the money to spay, neuter or medically treat the cats she took in. It seems that she continually ran an ad in the neighborhood newspaper making cats and kittens available for adoption, no fee or contribution required. Four years earlier

Faye called the number in the ad and was told to pick up Charles at a veterinarian's office. He was there for shots and castrating. Needless to say, the cat lady's instructions were not followed out to the letter, and Faye received her new charge as a whole male cat, complete and ready for action. It seemed an act of fate, and she didn't want to tamper with it. Besides, she preferred the cat that way.

Life with Charles was a pleasant existence for a woman alone. He was good company. When Faye returned home every day from her job at the neighborhood movie theater where she was a cashier, she fixed dinner for Charles and herself. After a brief cleaning of the apartment they would snuggle up together on the sofa and watch television, listen to the FM radio, or read a newspaper. Charles seemed to enjoy the closeness and often slept in a sitting position. This was their daily routine unless he heard some intruder penetrating his territory out back. His eyes then would open wide, his muscles would tense, and he'd leap to the windowsill to spot the troublemaker. On these occasions Faye was thoughtful enough to open the window and allow Charles out to do what he had to do. He always came back in an hour or two and tapped at the glass pane. Faye patiently waited for that tapping and let the cat back in for the night. They had been together four years, and weekdays were pretty much like that. Saturday and Sunday often varied because Faye had to work different shifts each weekend. She had to work one night a week either on Saturday or Sunday. Whenever she worked at night, Charles was not put out that day or night. The gray cat never adjusted to that idea and always asked to go out anyway.

It was on a Saturday that Faye was to report to work at 4:00 in the afternoon and work through that evening, including the special midnight horror show that she last saw Charles. He had insisted all day on being allowed out. Faye said no and said it quite firmly, but the big cat almost always got his way if he nagged her enough. Finally she weakened at about 2:30 that afternoon and told him to come back in one hour, just before she was to leave for work. When 3:30 came and Charles did not appear at the window, Faye decided to leave for work with great reluctance. She left his dinner outside on the fire escape and muttered that it would teach him a good lesson to wait out in the chilly night air for her to come home.

Faye's back was stiff and her eyes were slightly strained when she got home that night. Her fingers were gray from handling money and she felt in need of a bath. The crowd at the theater was large and noisy, and she had a headache. They pushed and shoved and argued with each other about who was first or next or allowed in front of others. It was good to be home. She kicked off her shoes, washed her hands, and put up some water for tea. While the TV was warming up, she casually went to the window where she expected to see a repentant Charles waiting for her forgiveness. He was not there. The food in his dish was never touched. Her head began to throb and she was annoyed.

By the next day, Faye was grief-stricken. Charles had simply vanished. After ten days it appeared that she would never see him again. Faye Jackson mourned for that cat as if he were her closest relative.

T. S. Eliot claimed that cats must have three different names. There is the name the family uses daily and then one that's peculiar and dignified. But then there is one name that is known only to themselves. Such must have been the case for Charles. This cat not only had other names but other lives, other people, and other homes. It all began when Faye Jackson, the first one to bring him to the neighborhood, allowed him to wander outdoors while she was at work. He immediately scouted the fire escape of the building next door. On the third floor landing, he peered in on a large man lifting weights. He was pressing seventy-five pounds in sets of five repetitions. The gray cat sat outside his window and watched the weight lifter until he caught his attention.

Avery Brown was a former marine who was in New York studying to be an actor. He worked all night in the Wall Street offices of one of the largest banks in the country. His job was entering negotiated checks into a computer system. He was really a glorified typist. He didn't like the work, but it paid well and gave him his days so that he could look for acting jobs. In two years he had not had one nibble. All of his frustration went into his barbells.

On that fateful day that the gray cat sat outside his window, Avery's phone rang and his acting career began. Avery was convinced that it was because of the cat. He looked for him the next day and opened his window when Charles appeared. The gray cat was eagerly taken inside and given another home. He wore no collar or ID tag, so Avery assumed that he was a stray. Avery immediately gave his new pet a name. From henceforth he was to be known as Booth.

It was a nice life that "Booth" was beginning to carve out for himself. He left the warmth and comfort of Faye in the morning and showed up for a late brunch with Avery, who also liked having a part-time cat. Luckily, he felt the same as Faye Jackson, only he never insisted on restraining the cat at all. Whenever and whatever Booth wanted to do was okay with him. After all, you never want to restrain a good-luck charm.

It wasn't long afterward that "Booth" hopped up to the fifth floor of Faye's building and began nosing about outside the fire escape. His sensitive pads could feel a strange but pleasant vibration from the metal platform outside this window. It was created by the lower notes of a piano being pounded somewhere inside the apartment. The cat's sensitive hearing picked up the tune, "Waltzing

Matilda," and began meowing along as he rubbed his chin
against the glass. Suddenly the music stopped, the shade
went up with a flap, and Marjorie Stockbridge peered
out at the cause of the disturbance. You could almost
hear violins and saxophones. It was love at first sight.
The thirty-year-old Australian girl opened her window
and reached for the gray cat like a parched traveler at
an oasis. He was instantly dubbed "Quakka" as he deli-
cately nibbled the lox off half a toasted, buttered bagel.

Marjorie was new in the country and had spent all
she had to get here. The buxom Australian was a post-
graduate student in anthropology at Columbia University
and held down a part-time job at the Museum of Natural
History. She worked in the book and gift concession as
a clerk but had great expectations. Between classes, her
job, and her studies, she rarely, if ever, went out. And so,
Quakka was a most welcome visitor. On his first visit he
allowed her to hug and squeeze him, but he jumped to
the windowsill at the first opportunity. "Oh," she said.
"You're a traveling man, are you? Okay. It's a deal. You
come and visit whenever you like, Quakka. I just love
you."

Across the back courtyard and up three landings of
the dark brown building were two rubber plants, a potted
geranium in bloom and something long, thin, and wiry
hanging over the sides of the planter. The plants were
taking the sun and seemed an open invitation for a cat in
need of a stomach settler. With nimble-footed alacrity
the gray cat took the steps two at a time and began
chomping on the green leaves sixty seconds after he
spotted them. The window rose swiftly and unexpectantly
catching Quakka by surprise. A muscular pair of arms, one
of which bore a tattoo of an anchor on it, reached out
and snatched up the cat by the scruff. This was a tough
tomcat but the arms that held him were so strong that
he was absolutely helpless. The window shut and a harsh

face peered into his as he was yelled at for the first time in his life.

Willie Boyle fought professionally in the middleweight division for nine years before he gave it up. Now he was an all-night counterman at a popular delicatessen. He was famous for his speedy delivery of cold-cut sandwiches and vast knowledge of boxing trivia. Willie was something of a legend.

He was very particular about his plants and didn't appreciate some stray cat chewing up his geranium. Sally Boyle intervened in behalf of the squirming cat and convinced her husband that he was a prehistoric brute to mistreat a defenseless animal in such a manner. With a scowl and a protest, Willie put the cat down and walked away. The cat followed him and jumped on his lap as soon as he sat down on the battered old couch. Sally squealed a raucous laugh as the cat began licking Willie's hand. The poor sap never knew what hit him. He was completely taken over by the forward visitor and didn't have a chance. "Hey, Sally," he yelled, "What d'you got for this guy?" That very morning he was given eight ounces of the best sliced corned beef in New York City, a bath, and the name "Benny."

Benny had one other client in his Greenwich Village coterie, a cookbook writer on the ground floor of Willie Boyle's building. For some profoundly hidden reason, Janet Steadfast called him "Beverly." But a cat by any other name will still devour a cheese and walnut soufflé that collapsed in the middle.

And so it was a grand and varied existence that a backyard cat lived with five names, five families, and all the freedom he wanted. But Charles, Booth, Quakka, Benny, and Beverly were all the same vulnerable animal—just a cat on the loose, tiptoeing through the lives of many people who loved him, needed him, and completely misunderstood his needs. The cat died in traffic and caused as much grief as he did pleasure, only fivefold. Charles, Booth, Quakka, Benny, and Beverly simply disappeared from the lives of those who loved him. They knew as little of his death as they knew of his life.

———————————◆———————————

From the cats' point of view, they never run away from home. They simply explore or expand their territory. The desire to roam about is natural to all cats including wild and domestic species. Both female and male cats wander throughout their range, but the male will wander farther and with more frequency. In the wild, roaming is done primarily to hunt for food. Because domestic cats living with human families do not have a need to hunt for survival purposes, they wander off to delineate territory, to establish their own ranges, to mate, and to defend all these gains. It is one of those practical jokes of nature that the charade of "wild behavior" be played out by cats that haven't the slightest knowledge of life in the raw. Because a domestic cat always knows on which side its paw is buttered, it will always return home, God willing.

Charles was a cat with too much freedom. Life in the city is in many ways as dangerous or worse than life in the wild. Here was a pet with five owners, and yet not one of them knew of the others because they would not assume the full responsibility for the animal's well-being. All were well intended, and yet the cat died. He was happy and he had it made. The cat had the best of all possible worlds. But the reality is that his ability to explore a world he didn't fully understand killed him. It is hard enough to find a street-wise human, let alone a cat with a virtuoso sense of survival.

Paul Leyhausen, the German ethologist and world's great authority on cats, has said there is probably no such thing as a truly solitary animal. Each individual periodically meets his neighbors at boundaries or at crossroads. This helps to develop a loose-knit social order with a degree of tolerance if there is no direct competition for a mate or for the same kill. So, even a solitary, independent cat leaves his lair and allows himself to make contact with the larger world around him. Charles was not disloyal to his primary owner, Faye Jackson. He simply expanded his territory by accepting the kindness of strangers. Domestic cats are much more gregarious than many people suspect and will enthusiastically allow themselves to be fussed with and given food by strangers, providing they are handled gently and affectionately.

It should be taken as a caveat by pet owners who love their cats. If given half a chance, their cats will sooner or later wander off to see what's beyond the horizon. There is very little danger that the pet cat will not return home unless fate intervenes. The wandering cat is always in danger of attack from natural enemies, the elements, natural booby traps (such as abandoned wells or sharp sticks poking out of the ground), cruel humans, or auto traffic.

The cat that wanders away for several days only to return home is behaving as a normal, healthy feline. It is part of their genetic composition to do this. It is up to the human caretaker to prevent the animal from getting loose. Although some cat owners feel strongly on the subject of tampering with the animal's sexuality, there can be no doubt of the value to society and benefit to the animal if it is spayed or castrated.

The added benefit to sexually neutering pet cats is that they are not likely to wander very far from home. For the romantic anthropomorphizer of pets, it will seem cruel or unnatural to alter cats or dogs, for that matter. But weighing the harsh realities of the disadvantages of sexually potent animals against the violation of one's fantasies about pets, there can be no question that neutering is the best thing. In most cases, a neutered pet confined within its home will live a longer, happier life than a free-roaming, sexually potent one.

All cat owners must understand that even their domestic house pets are part of a group that is considered to be the most highly developed of all the predators. The cat family, or Felidae, has evolved over the past ten million years into the most talented group of hunters on earth. With highly proficient olfactory (smell) apparatus, vision, and hearing, with great physical stamina and prowess, the entire range of the cat family has proven itself to be most formidable to all creatures great and small.

Is it little wonder then that even the smallest of the Felidae, the domestic house cat, is inclined to leave the tranquility of a secure home for an occasional outing in wild unknown territory. The veneer of domestication and sociability in the house cat is so thin that the slightest brush with freedom seems to bring into play the instincts of millions of years. Cats will chase, catch, kill, and (if hungry) eat rodents and insects. They will establish their hunting ranges, inner territories, paths, lairs, resting places and sunning spots in a very short period of time. They will fight for their territory and challenge all competition for the mating rights of an available female and do so to the death, if necessary. All this can be accomplished by the smallest of house cats, if given the opportunity. A cat that is allowed to roam free will inevitably leave home for a while, only to return with a new mystery about its secret life. Is the cat any crazier to leave than the human who allows it to leave?

CHAPTER NINE

THE BEAT GOES ON
(Aging)

Cats

Pet owners live with the constant fear that someone or something will take their dog or cat away. Ironically, preventing catnapping and running away from home is not difficult. Warding off old age and ensuing death is impossible. Regarding an older cat as if it were an "old" cat is how some pet owners play into their own worst fears. Because we accept stereotypical concepts of old age, we tend to regard our pets as old dogs or cats by doing some calculation on a pocket computer and then treating the animals based on some numbers game.

The old formula for comparing human/pet aging was to consider one cat year equal to seven human years. Therefore a five-year-old cat was considered the equivalent of a human being of thirty-five years. This theory begins to break down if the cat is eighteen years old. It would then be the equivalent of a human one hundred twenty-six years old. It just doesn't hold up. There is a newer theory that declares a six-month-old animal to be the equivalent of a ten-year-old human at the bottom of the scale. At the top of the scale a twenty-one-year-old animal is the equivalent of a hundred-year-old human.

The problem with this form of calculation is that the cat's real state of health, vigor, and youthfulness is ignored just like a sixty-five-year-old human who is forced to retire no matter what his condition. Most people agree that the average life-span of a cat is twelve or fourteen years, twenty years at the most. However, some cat experts feel that with proper diet, exercise, grooming, and medical attention, a cat does not have to be considered old until it has reached fifteen years and then should be able to live long past twenty.

Each cat is an individual and must be evaluated as such. Old cats have a great deal in common with old people. Their eyesight and hearing diminish to some degree. They experience lapses of memory and some loss of intellectual competency and motor efficiency. The body begins to experience a general state of physiological and anatomical decline. They then become more susceptible to disease.

However, this decline begins much later for some than others and may occur only in very gradual stages. Thus, some older persons and older cats are much more vigorous than others the same age and must be treated accordingly. You must not start wringing hands and getting out the bed-pans and wheelchairs the minute your cat reaches nine years of age. Treating a healthy, happy animal as though it were two steps from the grave is to hasten that terrible event. When the time comes, your cat will tell you in no uncertain terms that she needs a different approach to her life-style. Don't behave like a programmed computer and automatically regard your cat as an old invalid when it just isn't so. This will create awful problems of its own, not the least of which is emotional upset for the animal.

Cash was something of a watchcat. She always sat on top of the cigarette machine, near the cash register. Like a billowing lion with a mane gone wild, she kept a sharp Persian eye on each customer to make sure the check was paid. She was large and rather elegant for restaurant work, but no one complained, least of all her humans, Marj and Barney Hauser. Her place of employment was The Eat Inn, which was one of those superdiners with all the chrome work on the outside. It was located along busy U.S. 40 near the Illinois-Iowa border. The diner paid its taxes in Iowa, but Marj and Barney paid their personal income taxes in Illinois because their house, which was just behind the super-eatery, was on the opposite side of the state line. They were a family of mixed loyalties.

Big cat that she was, Cash's cream-colored coat with its Persian elegance created a false impression of delicate, fragile temperament. Sitting there at eye level with each customer seemed to inspire honesty and a meticulous effort to pay the check. There was something in her gaze that let you know she was not a pussycat. And yet, there had never been one bad incident between Cash and a patron. She was highly effective in her work and had been at it since kittenhood, twelve years before.

The Hausers never planned on hiring a cat or living with one either. She just entered the restaurant on her own, following the heels of a trucker with an oversized raincoat. There was a muddy rain the morning she entered their lives. She was soaked and looked like a baby porcupine or woodchuck with matted fur revealing bare skin and splats of mud and some old stains of motor oil. Her face was wrinkled with the unhappy frown that only a Persian can express. Like a black mattress button, her nose was pushed in even farther than normal because of her discomfort and fear of discovery.

It was Bill the dishwasher who spotted her first, dried

her off with an old dish towel and gave her a bowl of
lentil soup. One by one the waitresses wiped her down
even more and stuffed little morsels of grilled cheese and
tuna salad into her mouth. Within thirty minutes she was
somewhat civilized looking and presented to Marj Hauser
at the register. Bill told her that he would keep her if they
wouldn't. Marj was not a sentimental woman, but she
was generous. There was something admirable about the
hardy young kitten who had somehow beaten the high-
way traffic, beaten the stray animals, beaten the cats
whose territory she had to cross, and even beaten the
terrible storm that had lasted for three days. Marj knew
this was a special cat and had the good sense to convince
Barney to let her stay.

For some cat reason, the little Persian liked the top
of the cigarette machine. Perhaps it was warm or perhaps it simply allowed her to be at eye level with her
benefactor, Marj, while she did her job at the cash
register. It is common knowledge among cat people that
the feline mentality appreciates high places from which
they can survey all the action.

Like any other kitten, Cash was a curious creature.
She would explore the storage areas, the large commercial kitchen, the rest rooms, the basement, and the dining
areas. On her third day there, while walking along the wall
of the lunch counter, just beneath the feet of the diners,
she began to make a fast run to the front whenever a customer moved to the cash register. At first everyone thought
it was cute. But once, when Marj had gone into the kitchen
to discuss something with Barney, a customer left his
table and went to the register. He could have gone out
without paying his check if the young cat hadn't followed
him to the little pay booth and jumped up onto the
cigarette machine. She began to meeow loudly, catching
the attention of Marj. From that day on, they called her
Cash and she had a job.

Cash more than pulled her weight at The Eat Inn. She was one hard-working animal. When she wasn't resting atop the cigarette machine, she followed every customer to the cash register, and that was a lot of mileage during a busy breakfast, lunch, or dinner period. Actually, this function was most useful during the off hours when everyone's guard was down.

Cash was also a goodwill ambassador. She greeted everyone who came into the diner. Sometimes she did it hopping up to the lunch stool closest to the door and sitting there, blinking at all who entered. She was a warm, friendly conversation piece to the regulars. There wasn't a trucker who came in that didn't chuck her under the chin or slip her a corner of hamburger. But her best and most important work came in the evening after Marj and Barney closed shop. In the beginning, they took Cash home every night to their comfortable seven-room house. But after her first heat, they both agreed she'd be better off in the diner. Cash preferred sleeping there. It was quiet and there was much work to be done. The Hausers never realized that they had mice coming in every night from the surrounding empty fields. So it was with mixed emotions that they looked down at six dead little squeakers the morning after Cash spent her first night in the diner. It was clear that Cash's services were as important at night as they were during the day.

Over the years, Marj and Barney came to cherish the animal who grew into a majestic cream-coated Persian and saw to it that she had the best medical care available. They put her on a diet when she was five years old because she had become fat. The veterinarian insisted that she reduce from 22 pounds to a svelte 15 and she did after much arguing with overly generous customers. Oh, yes. In her second year she underwent an ovariohysterectomy. It upset Barney to see her in heat without any gratification. He felt it was too frustrating for her, and kittens were out of the question. Marj never got upset when Cash went into season but wasn't too thrilled about the operation. The veterinarian explained that it would probably have a life-extending effect as well as end her estrus cycles and the frustration connected with them.

Time passed, dishes broke, the Hausers prospered and Cash became a much loved and admired cat with a following all her own. People driving from one end of the country to another purposely drove along U.S. 40 just to stop at The Eat Inn and say hello to Cash, the famous watchcat. As she got older, she become less active, with more time on top of the famous cigarette machine than on the floor. She never did relinquish her nocturnal duties as a rodent-control warden. Like her ancient ancestors guarding the Egyptian granaries, Cash patrolled the inner perimeter of The Eat Inn complex and kept mice out permanently.

It was Barney who first noticed that she was moving a lot more slowly than she used to and was less willing to follow customers around than before. Her eyes squinted a bit, and she even fell off the cigarette machine once while making a graceful leap. He and Marj briefly discussed the fact that the cat was now twelve years old and ought to take things easier. They started to notice little things about her that indicated she was an aging cat. Her footing was not as steady as it once had been and she seemed to sleep much more than ever. It was clear that her hearing had become slightly impaired because she responded only when someone spoke to her in a loud voice.

One evening a waitress gave the cat her cut-up pork chop and fat trimmings. It was Cash's favorite treat. She ate about half, walked away to a discreet corner of the floor, and regurgitated. This happened several times in the same month at about the same time that Marj noticed a slight leaking of urine dripping constantly from her.

Like nervous parents, Barney and Marj took her to her doctor for a complete physical and a frank heart-to-heart. Yes, the vet said, she was getting older. No, she didn't have anything terrible or fatal. He placed her on a special diet and informed the Hausers that her kidney function had slowed down with age, thus the drip of urine. It was not going to go away. However, he said cheerfully, Cash was in otherwise good health considering her age and had many good years in her. It was as if the couple did not hear him because they kept focusing on the fact that she had kidney trouble. With heavy hearts and wrinkled brows, they went home to sort it all out.

As they entered their small house, all three of them looked like Persian cats with their wrinkled brows and cheeks. They had dinner and over coffee decided that life in the restaurant was too hard for their old cat. It was time, they agreed, for her to retire and enjoy the good life. And so, to her surprise, Cash spent the night—the first in over eleven years—in the house behind the diner.

Morning came and both Marj and Barney dressed, gulped down some coffee, and dashed out to work. To her utter shock and surprise, Cash was left behind with a bowl of some special kidney diet next to a container of water. Her litter pan was set out on the floor in the bathroom, which they forgot to show her. Smart cat, she found it herself.

At 9:00 that evening, Marj and Barney came home, tired, not so energetic themselves, and slightly depressed. Their depression soon turned to anger when they walked into the house to find the lamp knocked over, the carpet clawed, and one drape shredded at the bottom. There was also a definite smell of cat feces around, but it was not in its own proper receptacle. Barney found it with the sole of his shoe on the kitchen floor, next to a puddle of urine. They finally found Cash sitting in the dark under the stove.

They cleaned up the house and never said a word to the reclusive cat. It was as if she was not talking to them anymore. Actually, she came out of hiding after an hour and arrogantly marched into the living room, jumped on the mantel and let her tail hang over as she turned her thoughts inward.

Although they did not come home to a viciously destroyed home every night, the Hausers always found one minor bit of destruction. On Tuesday an ashtray had been knocked over and broken. The cushion of the sofa had been soiled on Wednesday because Cash chose to sit on it as she dripped. Thursday, she missed the litter box and used just part of it. Although Cash had never been a demonstratively affectionate cat, she did have her warm moments. But there wasn't the slightest display of affection or body contact between herself and the Hausers. Their feelings were terribly hurt.

On Friday morning they arose to the sound of the cat's sneezes. They took one look at her and knew she was very ill. There were liquid discharges from her nose and eyes. She had not touched any food in her bowl and she was obviously listless. Barney began to sneeze. He didn't feel too hot either. Marj shook her head and made a pot of strong coffee. They each went to their respective doctors. Barney and Cash were both down with a respiratory virus and were sent home to bed. They were given antibiotics and told to get plenty of rest. Cash's doctor noticed her changed mental state and commented on it. Barney told him about retiring the cat from work and bringing her into the house. No good, suggested the vet.

For six days man and cat loafed around the house working on getting better. Cash was still not her old self, but at least she was behaving. On the following

Saturday Marj decreed that Barney was well enough to return to work, but on a very limited basis. The same went for the cat.

Cash was taken out of retirement and set up on her old pedestal, the cigarette machine. They equipped it with a rubber sheet and lifted her down whenever she stood and stretched. The stubborn cat still insisted on jumping up there herself and maintained her nocturnal duties in the mouse department. Nobody could tell if she was still capable of catching any, but it made her happy. As fas as anyone knew on U.S. 40, Cash's gold watch was still a long way off.

There can be no doubt that the aging process is hastened or retarded by a combination of physiological, psychological, and sociological factors. We define aging as a physical change in the structure of cells, organs, or entire bodies of living organism. The aging process begins in mammals with the attainment of full maturity and continues until death. When the aging process is hastened, the animal becomes more susceptible to disease and consequently less capable of recovery.

Cash was assumed to be "old" and on the verge of infirmity because of her age and various minor impairments in her physical capacities. As an act of love and concern, Cash's owners retired her from a life of usefulness and activity. It was their most sincere desire to assure her longevity by making her remaining days effortless and free from physical strain. The net result was to create an emotional upset so severe as to have behavioral consequences and then physical breakdown. The change of life-style had the exact opposite effect from what the Hausers desired. Had they not had the good sense to reverse their decision, the cat might have speeded up the aging process and died fairly soon.

When a wild felid such as a mountain lion or puma becomes too old to defend its range, it must reduce the parameters of that range and maintain only the area that it can control. As territory diminishes, so does the food supply. Inevitably, a young challenger will appear to fight for the range or to drive off the old tenant. Without a territory, the old cat will soon perish.

A cat's relationship to its home is of greater importance than it is to its human family. This is due to the innate attitude toward territory. It is a genetically organized feeling and has significant ramifications for the cat owner. With rare exceptions, we cannot change a cat's home from one place to another and expect it to remain calm and content. Add to this the change of status, environment, population, and physical activity, and you have enough factors to induce a total nervous collapse. These were the nature of the changes made in the life of Cash.

Once she was removed from her range and territory of twelve years, removed from the many friendly people she was used to, removed from her job, she became disoriented. She experienced a tremendous emotional upset placing her body in a state of stress which is the enemy of the old and infirm. If anything will quicken the aging process, it is hyper-emotionalism and physical stress. All of Cash's body resources were being drained. Her instincts told her she was in grave jeopardy because she lost her territory. It did not matter that Marj and Barney were still there looking after her. It is quite likely that the destructive activity in their house was the result of serious but futile escape attempts. The failure to remain clean and housebroken may have been a desperate attempt to claim territory or a result of stress. We should rule out anger or revenge—that would be too simple.

Aging cats do not necessarily have to die at age nine,

twelve, fourteen, or fifteen years. With care, emotional harmony, and a bit of genetic luck a cat should live well into its second decade.

Older cats must not be removed from their homes if they are expected to remain emotionally undisturbed. Their routines must remain the same where possible, never varied in any radical way or to any great degree. Diet is not a serious matter for an aging cat. A well-fed cat need not have any dietary changes unless there is disease, in which case a veterinarian will recommend required changes. Older cats may eat less than usual or more than usual. Neither situation is desirable. A vitamin and mineral supplement is useful. Consult your veterinarian.

Do not restrict your cat's physical activity in play or in its routine indoor journeys. Its body will dictate to him what he can and cannot do. Naturally, if he cannot make those high jumps anymore, a little help from a friend can avoid a broken bone even if there is a slight loss of pride. There is no greater life-extending factor for an aging cat than frequent medical attention. Every six months is not too frequent for physical checkups for a cat over ten years old.

Very old cats sometimes experience something similar to human senility. They will hear things and see things that aren't there. There may even be temporary memory losses of people, places, and things. A senile cat may suddenly chase an imagined friend, foe, or prey animal. This is a foggy mental plateau from which there is no retreat. If it does not impair the cat's physical well-being, there is no reason why he cannot go on with his life, enjoying his delusions and fantasies. Euthanasia is the last resort and is a humane consideration when the animal is in pain or cannot function physically. Because all of our dear pets live only one day at a time with not the slightest concept of the next day, a peaceful, merciful end holds no fear for them. When a cat finally beds down and the day has been satisfying in all ways, he succumbs to a deep sleep with no thoughts of waking up. Each waking morning of his life is a surprise that he never expected.

Dogs

Dogs seem to get old suddenly. One day they're playing fetch, and the next day they're limping with arthritis as you notice the gray fur on their snouts for the first time. They become cranky, cantankerous, and downright unpleasant. Older dogs seem harder to get along with, less tolerant, and even snappish. One of the principal aspects of canine aging is anxiety, which causes emotional problems that do have bad effects. But those problems can be alleviated and, indeed, some dog owners have an intuitive understanding of this. They manage to keep their dogs happy and stable for their entire lives.

Most dog owners never realize that old age has caught up with their pets until there is some sign of illness or physical impairment. This is unfortunate because life can be prolonged and the quality of life maintained if the animal is cared for with intelligence and understanding. That requires an understanding of the aging process, how it works, and what to do for the animal as time passes.

Although it is hard to believe, the aging process begins in the average-size dog when he is six or seven years old. This is when full maturity peaks and the metabolism slows down. Cell reproduction begins to falter. The body's skeletal and muscular tissue density begins to slowly reduce in quantity and is gradually replaced by fluids. This means a lessening of the body's capacity to perform its various physical and chemical functions. Your dog may eat more but get less nutritional benefit from his food. Water and fat may accumulate in his body while actual tissue reduces to as little as two-thirds its youthful density. His body may gain weight but actually become smaller. It is, in a word, middle age.

Needless to say, a middle-aged dog, like a middle-aged

human, has many, many good years of productivity and happiness available when life is lived sensibly and with a degree of moderation or else the home mortgage business would fail. However, the aging process takes its toll and makes it necessary to place certain limits on physical activities, behavior, and, where possible, abrasive environmental influences. With these slight restrictions, life can be sustained in a reasonable state of health, and your dog can enjoy his full potential of normal longevity.

The older dog cannot be expected to live a full and healthy existence if he is placed in a state of continual anxiety. Anxiety may be a greater killer of older dogs than all sicknesses because it can induce any and all other sicknesses. It is the equivalent to living in a disease-ridden environment. Eventually the animal will succumb to disease and fail to rally the proper immunological defenses to survive. The will to live can exist only when there is a reasonable opportunity to survive. If the cause or causes of anxiety are not removed, then there is no hope for survival, and the will to live disappears.

The causes of anxiety in the older dog are varied, and most are obvious. However, there is an anxiety inducer that few dog owners fully appreciate, and that is the disruption of the normal routine.

———————◆———————

Life was about as perfect as it gets for the Stoner dog. He came from a fine line of Belgian sheepdogs with several champions in his pedigree. His founding stock originated in Europe and was one of the aspects of his pedigree that made his breeder brag the most. At first Charles Stoner hesitated to bring home to his family of six a dog with a better lineage than his own. How could he introduce a dog, albeit a cute puppy, as grand as Baron Noire Compagnon de Brugge to his very small children. The breeder wanted his friend Stoner to have this pup because he had a slight fault in his hind legs which would make him wrong for the show ring. The dog was an altogether perfect specimen with that one exception, and the breeder didn't have the heart to destroy him. Stoner decided he could take the puppy if it was okay to call him Blacky. The breeder agreed and it was arranged. Stoner also agreed to void the dog's American Kennel Club papers to discourage any possible mating. It was the breeder's request that the dog not sire any puppies because of his fault.

And so, Blacky started out with a rain check and went to the city to live with Charles and Marion Stoner and their four kids: Lisa, Robert, Fred, and Chuck. Things couldn't have turned out better. The children were all hands, arms, and cheeks as they almost loved their new pet to death. Blacky was in heaven. He was four months old when they got him, so he grew up with his four young pals.

Blacky turned into a large seventy-pound dog with a rugged, solid body. For a while he seemed taller than Chuck, the youngest of the children. Actually, he never was taller. The children became his special responsibility along with the nine-room house and the front and back lawns. Over the years he protected them, guided them in the right direction (quite literally), and took no nonsense.

Blacky was a serious decision-maker of a dog with herding instincts and a firm sense of territory. His size and his color settled all disputes with strangers whom he treated with an aloof air of *prove yourself worthy of my trust*. Blacky had a great bark and a running technique. Once someone was introduced to the bright, energetic guardian, he was forever remembered and allowed to advance to the house. It was then up to Marion to allow entrance into the house or not. Even then, the dog, a consummate protector, sat himself somewhere close by his mistress just in case he was needed.

His relationship with the children varied. Although Blacky had a definite air of superiority, he did not push the dominance business. The animal perceptively knew enough never to confront the issue with all of the youngsters, especially those who were already in their early teens when he was a puppy. Lisa, the eldest of the four, took him over from the very beginning. At thirteen, the girl mothered the little dog. His little, vulnerable body needed help going up stairs and adjusting to street traffic. His need for affection and assurance triggered an instinct in her that had disappeared with her last great doll. If Blacky had the key to anyone's heart, it was Lisa's. But as he grew into a juvenile and then adult dog, she changed her manner with him accordingly. She took no funny business and took him in tow. She was the only one in the family who could give him that self-doubt feeling that made his ears lie flat on top of his head. "Did you do this? Okay, Blacky, no chicken for you tonight." But when the tone of her voice changed to "You are the dearest person and I love you," his eyes glistened and his tongue panted with slurping joy.

Robert was twelve when Blacky was a puppy. The youngster was a big reader, and his approach to pet ownership was to acquire a book about obedience training and take charge with a book in one hand and a leash in the other. It took him seven or eight months to finally accomplish what the course promised in six weeks. By the third month, the playful dog began to take the boy seriously when he was yanked off his feet by the leash during a contest of wills. That was the first and last time he ever confronted Robert. Robert took on the air of a dominant member of the family, and it made the dog feel secure. As long as someone took on that responsibility the dog was satisfied. One always had the feeling that Blacky could have demoted Robert anytime he wished. There was a dignified, loving relationship between the two, and it lasted throughout their lives.

Dignity flew out the window when it came to young Fred and younger Chuck. The two boys, ten and six years old when Blacky was a puppy, were very involved with practical tricks, toilet humor, and using the dog as an occasional chemistry experiment, an extra in their games, a confederate in their kid crimes. Fred was always leading Chuck astray and drawing him into his pranks and secret activities. Little Chuck adored his older brother and followed him everywhere. This worried Blacky. He spent what seemed a lifetime finding the two of them and spoiling their best schemes—such as the time Fred wanted to start the family car and drive it a few feet. He might have hurt himself, Chuck, the car and perhaps someone out on the street.

The two boys entered the car like commandos. The keys had been left in the ignition. Blacky became instantly primed when he saw them moving in a crouched position. He slowly rose as he watched them intensely. They opened the car door and slipped inside. This violated the dog's sense of routine. He knew that the boys never went into the car by themselves. As they turned the key and attempted to get the car started without being noticed, the dog dove off the porch in a breathless leap and began attacking the door on the driver's side. His barking was loud and urgent, almost vicious. The light on the porch flicked on, and Charles and Marion came running out to see what was the matter. Fred and Chuck were yanked out of the car and sent to bed immediately. They lost their swimming privileges for the month of July. Blacky got to sleep on Marion's side of the bed where her hand occasionally touched his head as she slept. That was the finest reward the dog had ever been given.

In the cold months, during the day when everyone was either at school or at work, Blacky's job was Marion. He followed her from room to room as she kept the house clean and straight. When she did the laundry, he would sit by the vibrating washing machine and look at her as if he understood everything she said to him. If Blacky could have written a book, he could have told of every emotion and secret thought, wish, and complaint that the lady of the house had. He heard it all. He listened better than a hairdresser and kept his mouth shut, too. She loved him. Marion could not imagine a world without her true and loyal friend and confidant.

For Charles, Blacky was the thread that kept the family talking to each other when they were upset or not seeing each other very much. Lisa was dating several boys when she was not doing homework. Robert was busy winning a science award in Middle School, and even the younger boys were deep into their school life. Marion was involved in the activities of her various community groups doing volunteer work and organizing action groups for a traffic light here and a crossing guard there. There was never enough time for Charles to see the pro football game, clean out the garage, or cut the grass at the same time. He settled for a frequent walk with the dog. The two of them explored every square inch of their neighborhood for hours every weekend. Theirs was also a special relationship.

Over the years, Charles kept his word to Blacky's breeder and never had the dog mated. They had seriously considered having him altered but decided against it. As Chuck (known by his friends as Charles) said, "for religious reasons."

Lisa went to college, graduated, began a career as a teacher, and then married. At age twenty-seven she became pregnant. Robert was an industrial engineer and lived in his own apartment at the other end of the city. At twenty-four, Fred was a sergeant in the Air Force and stationed somewhere in Texas. He called home often—collect. Young Charles was still at home in his room taking on the demands of Psychology One in his junior year at the university. The class was up to *symptoms of abnormal psychology* and Charles was convinced he had everything from schizophrenia to erotomania. Charles and Marion became mom and dad and they were doing fine with the exception of an occasional backache and some sciatica. Blacky was fourteen years old.

The great old dog moved much more slowly than he did before. He was still a vigorous protector, but the deliverymen obeyed his instructions more out of respect for a senior dog than any other reason. He had a slight limp in his right hind leg from a brush with a moving car, and there was much gray in his dulled coat. The veterinarian cut the dog's rations to almost half of what they once were, and his running days were over. But Blacky still followed Marion around from one room to another as she tended to the routine of her much-loved home. Charles still took the old guy out for their weekend strolls around the neighborhood, but never for more than two or three or sometimes four blocks. By the time they got home, the old dog was obviously fatigued.

Lisa and her husband moved back into the family home while they had their baby. It was a joyous event for everybody, including Lisa and her old dog Blacky. Over dessert one evening, Charles became a little expansive and said he wanted to give his future grandchild something fine, something valuable. A dog, he declared. By God, the child shall have a dog and all of the pleasures and rewards that go along with it. He looked over to the far corner of the dining room and looked at Blacky, sitting and quietly participating in silence. Charles experienced a dreadful thought and felt a deep hole in his stomach. "Yes," he said, "we'll get a puppy for the new baby."

A baby boy was brought home from the hospital six weeks later. He was named James. The next day Charles went to see his friend who bred Belgian sheepdogs and came home with a six-month-old female who had already been dubbed Adelaide. Everyone enjoyed calling her Addy. She was an instant hit. Blacky turned away with indifference.

Between the excitement of baby James and Attagirl Addy, Blacky was somewhat taken for granted, except by Marion who still allowed him on her side of the bed. For three weekends in a row, Charles forgot about his constitutional with Blacky. He was doing what every proud grandfather did; he took his grandson around the neighborhood in his carriage, offering cigars and showing photographs to all the neighbors. Blacky stationed himself out on the porch but refused to chase after the preoccupied man.

Addy was a very friendly dog and did her best to strike up some rapport with the crusty old herder. She made the mistake of approaching him while he was at his food bowl one morning. He let out a deep hissing growl that hadn't been heard from him since he chased a cop with a drawn gun off their lawn ten years ago. The younger dog froze and got bitten on her upper lip. She bled slightly. The family was upset, and even Marion hollered at him. Blacky just slunk off to a corner of the basement and stayed out of sight for the rest of that day.

A month passed by, and Blacky became surly and something of a recluse. His gaze seemed focused inward. He no longer solicited loving pats and affectionate glances. He even stopped following Marion around on her housecleaning rounds and failed to show up for washday. She became hurt, upset, and worried when the dog refused to sleep in their bedroom anymore. When they let him, he slept out on the porch. Charles was becoming disturbed by Blacky's behavior and was determined to work it out. He decided to leave Blacky and Addy alone in the house for several hours one afternoon and allow them to work

out their differences, including who was top dog and anything else that was bothering them. It was risky but worth
a try. That Sunday everyone cleared out and left Addy
staring at them as they left. Blacky arose from the floor
as soon as he heard the car door slam and walked out of
the room. Addy watched him leave and followed him.
The time dragged. Charles rushed home one hour earlier
than he had set. He couldn't take the pressure. He was
worried about Adelaide's safety. When they returned
home they were amused to find that Addy was curled
up asleep in one corner of the living room and Blacky
was curled up asleep in the corner of the kitchen. "Nothing happened," said Marion in a dejected tone. "Well,"
said Charles, "we'll just have to live with this situation as
best we can. We owe Blacky too much to take it out on
him now."

Two days later, Marion woke up in the morning and
found Blacky on the floor next to her bed. He did not
move. She knew instantly. The family was gently informed that Blacky had left them. He was buried in a state
park somewhere in the woods that he and Charles had
explored on one of their Sunday walks.

It took three or four weeks before the heaviness lifted
around the Stoner house, and once again young master
James took the spotlight when he could from Addy. The
black dog got all stirred up during a session of exuberant
play with young Charles, who had taken time off from
his studies. For him it was like old times romping around
with another sheepdog. In an unexpectant fit of brief
hysteria, Adelaide snapped and caught Charles on the
thumb. He yelled out in pain and moved away. There
was a bit of blood. Lisa chastised the dog and made her
leave the room. She went to the kitchen, walked up to her
food bowl, and devoured the contents in one quick gorg-
ing. In a few seconds, she began to regurgitate.

The next day Charles took her to the veterinarian

for a checkup. She didn't look too good, and her behavior was different. Nobody could understand it.

The examination took exactly four minutes when the vet asked, "How old is this girl?"

Charles shrugged and answered, "Eight months, I think. Why?"

The vet smiled and said, "Well, she's a bit young, but it'll be okay."

"What will?" asked Charles.

The vet's answer was a shock. "Pregnant," exclaimed Charles. "Pregnant?!!" He thought about it for a minute and then smiled, too.

Together he and the doctor said, "Blacky."

Charles's chest began to push out, and something between a cry and a laugh escaped. "I'll be goddamned. Good for you, Blacky."

He went home with the dog, told everyone the astonishing news, and went out for a long walk. He didn't get home till after dark.

As old age catches up with our pet dogs, there is little or nothing we can do to prevent them from getting extra-sensitive to those things that never upset them in the past. This hypersensitivity is part of their nature. Wild dogs and wolves are acutely aware of their failing bodies. With the loss of physical prowess, diminishing eyesight or hearing comes the loss of pack status. A wolf whose teeth are no longer sharp enough to deliver the death blow to a prey animal may not be allowed to enter the hunt, and that means being consigned to eat what little has been left by the others.

A wolf that is not part of the hunt is eventually disenfranchised and left on his own as a "lone wolf." This is a death sentence. Wolves that are wounded, sick, or dying represent a threat to pack integrity. They hinder all aspects of pack existence including defense, hunting, and migration along with the prey animals. Wolves so afflicted are in great danger; at any time the pack may tear them to pieces as survival technique. As a leader of the pack becomes too old or infirm, he is apt to be challenged by a younger member for that position. This is behavior that has been genetically programmed into the animal. It exists in various degrees deep within the genes of all dogs.

It is little wonder then that our pet dogs become moody, grouchy, and hypersensitive as they get older. Dogs do not fear death (as indeed humans should not) because there is no frame of reference for so abstract a concept. However, there is an innate fear that along with old age comes a direct challenge from the social structure to his rights of territory, status, and life itself. Although an older dog's grumpiness may come from pain or discomfort, more likely it stems from some change in his routine that his owner did not recognize as a change.

Blacky was getting older. His family did the only thing that creates the greatest anxiety in old dogs. He was forced to live with and adjust to his replacement in the pack structure. Although it was not intentional, it was an extremely harsh change in the old dog's life even though the other dog was a young female and not a true challenge to his status. Blacky would have had enough to deal with having a grandchild enter the house, but another dog was more than his nerves could take. It was an attack on his entire nervous system and created a high degree of anxiety. As stated before, anxiety creates physical stress, and if prolonged, will cause collapse and even death. What was most notable about Blacky was the valiant effort to regain his position as the young, vigorous leader by asserting his sexual capacity with Adelaide. Sadly enough, it may have cost him his last bit of energy.

A dog pack can be likened to the human family or, in its

broadest sense, a national entity. If you are a member of the family or a nonrelated friend of the family, or a citizen of a country, you have various rights and privileges relative to your position in that structure. As long as you do not overstep your position or take that to which you are not entitled, you may live your life in relative peace and harmony. But, if you enter the territory of another pack, or attempt to join a strange pack without an invitation, or enter a country illegally, you become vulnerable to attack either by the pack leaders or by the law-enforcement officials of the offended nation. In large cities, teen-age gang warfare is caused by just such a social reality.

When a pack or a herd of animals becomes too populated for a territory to sustain, natural controls go into effect. Food obviously diminishes, so that hunger and sickness begin to thin out the density of population. Certain behavioral traits come into play that also achieve the desired goal. Some members of a pack or herd will break away, form a new group structure, and then emigrate in search of establishing another territory. Competition for the food and even the territory itself may take place within the social structure. This competition is in the form of a physical confrontation, with the winners remaining and the losers being sent off to wander and possibly die. The losers of such competitions are mostly juveniles, subordinates, the sick, and the old.

The next time you look down into the face of your aging dog, try to understand that some part of his or her brain has a coded message to be on guard and watch for changing signs in the environment. The answer to all your aging dog's emotional problems lies within the definition of the world *reassurance*. Do not change your older dog's routine at all, if possible. Give him or her as much attention and affection as in the past. If possible, give even more of yourself than before. Never leave the dog with strangers. Do not introduce another animal into the household as long as your pet is still living with you. Avoid overnight stays unless you take your dog with you. Try to avoid leaving the dog overnight at an animal hospital unless it is absolutely necessary. Dietary changes should be accomplished very gradually. Increase the number of times you groom your dog. This is a loving activity that not only serves as an opportunity to examine the animal for physical changes but allows you to physically express your feelings.

Reassurance soothes the aging dog and abates those primeval fears which cause so much irrational and unnecessary emotion. Talk to your dog in a gentle, loving tone of voice. Walk with him at a pace that makes sense for his body, not yours. Carry him upstairs, if necessary. Brush him gently every day. Do not subject an old dog to the rigors of very young children. Avoid loud noises. Be firm but not harsh. Communicate with him in some manner whenever something different is about to happen. Of course your dog cannot understand what you say in terms of words. But you'd be surprised how much is understood by the loving tone of your voice.

Meditation is a viable option for those who are interested in the therapeutic effects of this Eastern technique of relaxation and spiritual attainment. Members of all religions are now experimenting with meditation, and many physicians are also recommending it. Meditation for pets (PM) is easily practiced and offers an opportunity for reassurance—perhaps the best opportunity—that he is wanted, that life is good and that you still love him.

Remove yourself and the dog to a part of the apartment or house where you will not be disturbed for thirty minutes. Advise other members of the household that you do not want any noise or interference. Ask them to take your calls or answer the door. If you and the dog are alone, take the receiver off the hook.

Once the room is quiet, get on the floor so you're on the dog's level. If the animal is nervous or fidgety use a leash and collar. Seat yourself against a wall or piece of furniture and induce your dog to lie down next to you. Small dogs can even be placed in your lap. Flatten both of your hands and lay them over your dog's heart, which is found in the front of the torso, slightly behind the legs. Try to get a sense of his breathing pattern and allow your hands to rise and drop with his expanding and contrasting chest movements. This should be very pleasant for the animal. Few if any will resist.

Once your dog is calm, establish a visual rapport. Eye-to-eye contact is fine, but not as a direct stare. For some dogs, this is regarded as a challenge or an invitation to play. Maintain as much silence as possible except when the dog needs to be told that everything is fine. Align your breathing rate to the dog's and breathe together. Pet him slowly as you breathe in unison, keeping one hand over the dog's heart. You may look away or close your eyes and say soothing, loving things to him. You may even whisper his name.

Whatever you choose to do, be certain that it does not distract your dog and get him on his feet. If he gets up, reposition him and start over. Make him and yourself as comfortable as possible. For those who are experienced with meditation, do not be upset if you do not achieve the desired state of relaxation you are used to. This is for the inner state of the dog, not the human. You will know if you are succeeding.

Keep track of the time and break off the first session at fifteen minutes. Gradually extend the sessions until the dog is meditating for thirty minutes a day. Morning sessions are probably best if the dog must endure an entire day of nerve-wracking activities such as children and other distractions. Afternoons are also excellent for meditation. The time is not nearly so important as the level of relaxation and emotional well-being that is achieved. Communication of your love and assurance of his safety can be accomplished through this wonderful lifesaving activity.

The emotional problems of cats and dogs are best understood through the spectrum of animal behavior as it is determined by nature and circumvented by domestication. We have taken dogs and cats out of their natural habitat where their behavior makes sense, increased their population beyond the natural inclination, and demanded of them an adaptation to complex human society. In the humanization of Fido and the peoplizing of Tiger we have given our pets all of the emotionalism that goes along with the comforts and distortions of modern times. As we attempt to soothe our own inner turmoil, so must we help our four-legged alter egos, our mammalian cousins who have been pressed into service. The answer for them does not lie in primal scream therapy or Zen jogging. Pet owners must behave as responsible adults and help their friends with a truer understanding of animal behavior and their own role in creating the emotional problems of their pets. Thus equipped, we may look forward to a new kind of happiness where cats, dogs, and people are given the freedom to be themselves.

SUGGESTED READING

Dogs

Campbell, William E. *Behavior Problems in Dogs*. Santa Barbara, California: American Veterinary Publications, 1975.

Dangerfield, Stanley and Howell, Elsworth. *The International Encyclopedia of Dogs*. New York: Howell Book House, 1971.

Fiennes, Richard. *The Order of Wolves*. New York: Bobbs-Merrill, 1976.

Fox, Michael W. *Behavior of Wolves, Dogs and Related Canids*. New York: Harper & Row, 1971.

Howe, John. *Choosing the Right Dog*. New York: Harper & Row, 1976.

Judy, Will. *Puppies and Their Care*. Westchester, Ill.: Judy-Berner Publishing Co., 1972.

——. *Handling the Mating*. Westchester, Ill.: Judy-Berner Publishing Co., 1972.

van Lawick-Goodall, Hugo and van Lawick-Goodall, Jane. *Innocent Killers*. Boston: Houghton Mifflin Company, 1971.

McGinnis, Terri. *The Well Dog Book. The Dog Lover's Illustrated Medical Companion.* New York: Random House and The Book Works, 1974.

Mery, Fernand. *The Life, History and Magic of the Dog.* New York: Grosset & Dunlap, 1970.

Morris, Mark L., Jr. *Canine Dietetics.* Topeka, Kansas: Mark Morris Associates, 1975.

Pearsall, Margaret E. *The Pearsall Guide to Successful Dog Training.* New York: Howell Book House, 1973.

Pfaffenberger, Clarence. *The New Knowledge of Dog Behavior.* New York: Howell Book House, 1963.

Ryden, Hope. *God's Dog.* New York: Coward, McCann & Geoghegan, Inc., 1975.

Schaller, George B. *Golden Shadows, Flying Hooves.* New York: Dell Publishing Company, 1973.

Scott, John Paul. *Aggression.* Chicago: University of Chicago Press, 1958, 1975.

Scott, John Paul and Fuller, John L. *Dog Behavior: The Genetic Basis.* Chicago: University of Chicago Press, 1965.

Siegal, Mordecai. *The Good Dog Book.* New York: Macmillan Publishing Company, 1976.

Siegal, Mordecai and Margolis, Mathew. *Good Dog, Bad Dog.* New York: Holt, Rinehart & Winston, 1973.

——. *Underdog.* New York: Stein and Day, 1974.

Vine, Louis L. *Breeding, Whelping, and Natal Care of Dogs.* New York: Arco Publishing Company, 1977.

Winge, Ojvind. *Inheritance in Dogs.* Ithaca, New York: Cornell University Press, 1950.

Cats

Beadle, Muriel. *The Cat*. New York: Simon and Schuster, 1977.

Caras, Roger. *The Roger Caras Pet Book*. New York: Holt, Rinehart & Winston, 1976.

Ewer, R. F. *The Carnivores*. Ithaca, New York: Cornell University Press, 1973.

——. *Ethology of Mammals*. New York: Plenum Press, 1968.

Gaines. *Basic Guide to Canine Nutrition, Fourth Edition, With a Chapter on the Nutritional Requirements of Cats*. White Plains, New York: Gaines Professional Services, 1977.

Greer, Milan. *The Fabulous Feline*. New York: Dial Press, 1961.

Guggisberg, C. A. W. *Wild Cats of the World*. New York: Taplinger Publishing Company, 1975.

Immelmann, Klaus. *Grzimek's Encyclopedia of Ethology*. New York: Van Nostrand Reinhold, 1977.

Levinson, Boris M. *Pet-Oriented Child Psychotherapy*. Springfield, Illinois: Charles C Thomas, Publisher, 1969.

Leyhausen, P. *"Ver Haltensstudien an Katzen,"* Zeitschrift fur Tierpsychologie Beiheft, No. 2, 1956, pages 11–113.

McGinnis, Terri. *The Well Cat Book*. New York: Random House and The Book Works, 1975.

Manolson, Frank. *My Cat's in Love or, How to Survive Your Feline's Sex Life, Pregnancy and Kittening*. New York: St. Martin's Press, 1970.

Morris, Mark L. Jr. *Feline Dietetics*. Topeka, Kansas: Mark Morris Associates, 1976.

Phillis, J. W. *Veterinary Physiology*. Philadelphia: W. B. Saunders Company, 1976.

Raleigh, Ivor; Scott, Patricia; Jackson, Elizabeth and Oliphant. *Practical Guide to Cats*. London: The Hamlyn Publishing Group, Ltd., 1976.

Wilson, Edward O. *Sociobiology: The New Synthesis*. Cambridge, Massachusetts: The Belknap Press of Harvard University Press, 1975.

INDEX